WATER MONSTERS
SOUTH OF THE BORDER

BY DENVER MICHAELS

Cover design by Chris George Zuger of Megatron Creative +
Strategy.

info@megatroncreative.com

Special thanks to my daughter for providing all of the illustrations in this book.

To my wife.

Contents

Preface

My first book, *People are Seeing Something: A Survey of Lake Monsters in the United States and Canada* was a culmination of many years of research and study of the lake monster phenomenon. Canada and the United States are hotbeds for lake monster activity; my book covered over 60 creatures spanning thirty states and six provinces. This being said, the United States and Canada do not have the market cornered where lake monsters are concerned. Quite the opposite is true; lake monster and sea serpent sightings are worldwide—and always have been.

Concerning lake monsters outside of the United States and Canada, I had heard of Scandinavian monsters such as Storsjöodjuret long before I became familiar with many of the creatures I wrote about in my first book. The fierce creature's name means "the great lake monster." Likewise, I also had familiarity with several Russian water monsters long before writing my book—most notably, the Devil of Lake Labynkyr. Naturally, if North America is an epicenter of cryptid activity, then Russia should be too; after all, a land bridge connected present-day Russia with present-day Alaska in the remote past.

This book, though, is not about the lake monster phenomenon occurring on the Eurasian landmass; rather, this work will focus on the United States' neighbors to the south—Mexico, Central and South America, and the Caribbean.

I have always had a fascination with this part of the world, especially South America. Thinking of the Amazon Rainforest, and its seemingly never-ending canopy fills me with wonder. The canopy alone covers an area roughly 2/3 the size of the United States! The amount of water moving through the Amazon River and its tributaries is simply astounding. I can't help but wonder what kind of undiscovered life could be lurking in the waters and in the jungles.

I am not alone in my amazement. The vast, unexplored corners of the Amazon have stirred the imaginations of those who came before me. The wonder of the region has lured countless explorers—some of whom gave their lives.

In popular culture, the Amazon has been the setting for numerous films. The iconic Gill-man, better known as "The Creature," from the classic black and white movie, *Creature from the Black Lagoon*, is an

1

enduring reminder of how the Amazon stirs the imagination of mankind. Gill-man was a surviving humanoid amphibious creature from the Devonian Period who inhabited a lagoon in the remote reaches of the Amazon.

As with my first book, this work does not represent an exhaustive study or list, nor is it meant to. There are going to be creatures that are missed, "fall through the cracks," or simply get passed over. Complicating matters, for every cryptid that we know of, or think we know of, there are bound to be others that we do not. Such is the nature of the topic.

I sincerely hope that you will enjoy reading this book; I certainly had a lot of fun writing it! So, without further hesitation, let's take a trip south of the border, where much like persons in Russia, Scandinavia, Canada, and the United States—*people are seeing something in the water.*

Denver Michaels,

February 29, 2016

Chapter One: South America

Colossal Snakes of the Amazon

Sucuriju gigante, the controller, Camoodi, Cobra grande, black boa, Yacumama, Sachamama, giant anaconda—these names, and more—all interchangeable, refer to the enormous snakes that stalk the Amazon Basin.

The first reports of immense serpents reached the outside world through the testimony of early European explorers who ventured into the remote wilds of South America in search of riches. The tales of the explorers were corroborated by the legends of the natives. The legends state that there are snakes over 125 feet long lurking in the wilderness. Anyone who gets within 250 feet of these gargantuan snakes, enter their mouths—victims are "sucked in."[1] For this reason, indigenous people would blow into conch shells before entering the water in hopes of causing the creatures to reveal themselves—just in case one happened to be lurking nearby. You cannot be too careful when dealing with snakes over 100 feet long!

The massive, slithering giant, said to reach lengths exceeding 100 feet, is most commonly referred to as a "giant anaconda." This, however, is a misnomer; it is rare for anacondas to reach a length of 30 feet, much less the 130+ foot lengths that have been ascribed to these giants of the jungle.

The Amazonian giant snake is dark brown to black in color; quite different than the largest species of anaconda—the green anaconda. It is much, much larger too. Female green anacondas are larger than males. Females can reach a weight of 550 pounds and a length of 30 feet. Conversely, the "giant anaconda" as it is so often called, is said to reach weights of 5,000 kilograms, or 5.5 tons! They reportedly reach lengths of 40 meters, the equivalent of 131 feet. The goliath reaches a diameter of 2 meters, or 6.5 feet.[2]

The snake, which I will refer to as the Yacumama from here on out, has some distinctive features: it sports a large triangular-shaped head; eyewitnesses have reported horns, antennae, or some other type of protrusion on the snake's head; the creature also has very unique eyes that are large, and blue to bluish-green in color. In addition, the Yacumama's eyes are phosphorescent; when spotted at night, the creature's eyes have been mistaken for the navigational lights that are common to the boats that travel the Amazon.[3]

Mention of the bluish, phosphorescent eyes of the Yacumama brings to mind an interesting encounter. In 1929, a priest, Father Victor Heinz, was travelling at night on a river. Heinz saw a huge snake in the water. The snake had such large eyes—phosphorescent eyes—that Heinz initially mistook the snake for the navigational lights on a steamboat.[4]

Father Heinz had another encounter with the legendary Yacumama seven years earlier. Heinz was travelling along the Amazon River by canoe with several companions. He witnessed a massive snake whose visible portions were an estimated 80 feet in length. Heinz described the body of the snake as being as big around as an oil drum.[5]

The Most Famous Account

Perhaps the best-known account of a "giant anaconda" comes from the intrepid explorer Percy Fawcett (1867–1925). While canoeing near the confluence of the Río Negro and Río Abuna in 1907, Fawcett and his crew encountered a mammoth snake. Fawcett claimed to have killed the beast which measured and astounding 62 feet in length. The cover of his book *Exploration Fawcett*, published posthumously, bears a drawing of the encounter with the serpent.

Figure 1: Cover of Fawcett's book depicting the encounter with an enormous snake.

The following account is from *Exploration Fawcett*, compiled by Fawcett's son Brian from his letters, manuscripts, and log books. The book was published in 1953:

> We were drifting easily along on the sluggish current not far below the confluence of the Río Negro when almost under the bow of the igarité there appeared a triangular head and several feet of undulating body. It was a giant anaconda. I sprang for my rifle as the creature began to make its way up the bank, and hardly waiting to aim smashed a .44 soft-nosed bullet into its spine, ten feet below the wicked head. At once there was a flurry of foam, and several heavy thumps against the boat's keel, shaking us as though we had run on a snag.
>
> With great difficulty I persuaded the Indian crew to turn in shorewards. They were so frightened that the whites of their eyes showed all around their popping eyes, and in the moment of firing I had heard their terrified voices begging me not to shoot lest the monster destroy the boat and kill everyone on board, for not only do these creatures attack boats when injured, but also there is great danger from their mates.
>
> We stepped ashore and approached the reptile with caution. It was out of action, but shivers ran up and down the body like puffs of wind on a mountain tarn. As far as it was possible to measure, a length of forty-five feet lay out of the water, and seventeen feet in it, making a total length of sixty-two feet. Its body was not thick for such a colossal length—not more than twelve inches in diameter—but it had probably long been without food. I tried to cut a piece of the skin, but the beast was by no means dead and the sudden upheavals rather scared us. A penetrating, foetid odour emanated from the snake, probably its breath, which is believed to have a stupefying effect, first attracting and later paralysing its prey. **Everything about this snake is repulsive** (emphasis added).
>
> Such large specimens as this may not be common, but the trails in the swamps reach a width of six feet and support the statements of Indians and rubber pickers that the anaconda sometimes reaches an incredible size, altogether dwarfing the one shot by me. The Brazilian Boundary Commission told me of one killed in the Rio Paraguay exceeding 80 feet in length! In the Araguaya and Tocantíns basins there is a black variety known as Dormidera or 'Sleeper', from the loud snoring noises it makes. It is reputed to reach a huge size, but I never saw one. These reptiles live principally in swamps, for unlike the rivers, which often become mere ditches of mud in the dry season, the swamps always remain. **To venture into the haunts of the anaconda is to flirt with death** (emphasis added).

The Fawcett account is fascinating; however, the actual size of the snake that he shot has been widely questioned. The width of the snake is not proportionate with the length. However, Fawcett's writings are considered to be reliable; moreover, Fawcett himself makes mention of the fact that the snake was not as big around as it should have been when considering its length. If Fawcett was exaggerating the length of the snake, why wouldn't he exaggerate the width as well?

Other Notable Reports

In 1932, a massive snake was killed by the Brazilian Boundary Commission. The behemoth, which was an astonishing 4 feet thick and 105 feet long, was killed near the Venezuelan border. The animal's carcass was photographed and turned into a postcard.[6]

Figure 2: Is this photograph a hoax?

Many doubt the authenticity of the photograph—with good cause. It is hard to get a sense of scale, and the people in the background are blurry and only add to the confusion. The lack of scale makes the photograph unreliable as evidence.

In 1948, west of Manaus, Brazil, a gargantuan snake was captured as it was swallowing a steer. The bull was about half eaten at the time. The snake was tied to a tug and dragged downriver where it was shot to death with a machine gun. The snake was photographed and measured. It was said to be 2.5 feet wide and 130 feet long.[7]

In 1949, Joaquim Alencar photographed an enormous snake on the Río Abunã in Brazil. The photograph was published in *A Província do*

Pará, a Brazilian newspaper. It was claimed that the snake measured 45 meters (147 feet) in length. This estimate has been called into question; some skeptics claim that the photograph, although probably unaltered, was probably taken as very close range and perspective distorted its apparent gargantuan size.[8] The picture is shown below:

Figure 3: An enormous snake no doubt, but how big is it really?

In another account from the late 1940s, a man named Paul Tarvalho saw a snake come out from the water that he claimed was 150 feet long.

Two other noteworthy reports of large, albeit much smaller, anacondas occurred in the 1940s. Vincent Roth claimed to have killed a 34-foot-long anaconda in British Guiana. This account was not verified, but certainly seems plausible. In 1944, during a petroleum expedition in Columbia, an anaconda measuring 38 feet long was killed. Although both of these snakes are dwarves compared to the snakes that are the subject at hand, and most likely not even the same species, they are still larger—by quite a bit—than the largest verified anaconda and merit mention.

Along these lines, Raymond L. Ditmas, curator of reptiles at the Bronx Zoo in New York, offered a cash reward to anyone who could offer conclusive evidence for a snake measuring over 40 feet in length.

The reward was set at $1,000 in 1920, and grew to $50,000 over the years. The reward was never claimed.

Unique Traits and Abilities of the Yacumama

The Yacumama is a variant name of the gigantic monster snake that we have been discussing in this section. The name, Yacumama, roughly translates to "mother of the water." The mother of the water is certainly an appropriate term for such a colossal reptile.

The Yacumama has some characteristics that have gone unmentioned to this point. Of these, the snake is known to burrow deep underground and dwell there for long periods of time. It also sleeps or hibernates—possibly for years at a time.

Native folklore throughout the Amazon Basin mentions a massive snake that "carries its water with it." This is interesting; it is known to the locals that the Yacumama engorges itself with water. The Yacumama uses this water when it hunts; it is able to "shoot" a stream of water and knock monkeys out of trees, much like a high-powered water cannon. In fact, natives tell of a loud "booming" sound that carries through the jungle as the snake hunts. The Yacumama might also use its water shooting ability to help it burrow into the earth.[9]

The Nueva Tacna Incident

In 1997, an extraordinary event occurred in Nueva Tacna, Peru, a small village near Iquitos. What happened is truly awesome—an enormous snake that was hibernating beneath the ground awakened and made its way toward the Napo River. During its trek to the river, the giant left a trail of destruction 500 meters long and 20 meters wide (1,640 feet x 65 feet).[10]

According to witnesses, loud rumbling sounds accompanied the snake's movement toward the river. Additionally, though few witnesses were able to see the snake, they clearly saw the jungle floor move which displaced mud and uprooted trees. Carlos Manuyama, a local inhabitant, said, "the earth trembled as we were in the middle of an earthquake...we saw trees started to fly..."[11] Local villagers described the gouge in the earth left behind as large enough to drive a tractor through.

According to Maximo Inuacari, a fisherman who was sitting in his boat when the event took place, a loud rumbling sound accompanied the creature and it cut a trench into the ground as it approached the river. When the snake made it to the river, its massive body and force created a whirlpool which sank several boats.[12]

The news wire service *Reuters* reported the event in a headline titled "Monster Boa Size of Two Buses Reported by Terrified Village" on August 20, 1997. The report stated that a snake 130 feet long and 15 feet in diameter was responsible for the damage. Luis Iluma was one of the few who caught a glimpse of the creature. "It was black, very black," he said, and went on to state that it was the length of two passenger buses.

The incident was reported lightheartedly by many news outlets and skeptics tried to dismiss the damage as the result of soil degradation from torrential rains. However, the damage was localized to the path that villagers attributed to the snake.

Though the media may have mocked the villagers' belief that a Sachamama had awakened and destroyed a tract of land, the matter was taken seriously at the local level. At the request of the mayor, the military came in to survey the damage.

Discovery of the Yacumama

For over two decades, Mike Warner has studied reports throughout the world of colossal snakes. The retired lithographer from Northern Ireland was led to the accounts of Percy Fawcett in his research. Fawcett described trails over six feet wide that run through the jungle in his writings. These trails lead from water and abruptly terminate in the jungle.

Warner believed that if he could find the channels that Percy Fawcett wrote about, and prove their existence, then he may be able to prove the existence of the Yacumama as well. At a friend's suggestion, Warner made use of GoogleEarth™ imagery to study the area surrounding the confluence of the Napo and Amazon rivers. According to his son Greg, "we believed these creatures favor areas where two rivers meet as that provides them with two sources of food supply."[13] Moreover, during the course of Mike Warner's research, he learned of the Nueva Tacna incident. Warner predicted that the snake would relocate downriver at the next major confluence.

The GoogleEarth™ images of the area revealed irregular shaped channels leading from the water into the jungle where they ended. This closely matched the descriptions made by Percy Fawcett a century earlier. The confluence of the Napo and Amazon warranted further study.

Warner commissioned Digitalglobe and Europa Technologies to obtain satellite photographs of the area. Incredibly, the images revealed what Warner believed to be the shed skin of a large snake in one of the channels. At first glance, the skin appears to be a section of whitewater; however, there is no whitewater in that section of the jungle. In another image, a triangular shape is visible in a smaller channel. The triangular shape is eerily similar to the descriptions of the Yacumama's head.[14]

The Expedition

To prove the existence of the giant Amazonian snake, Mike Warner spent his entire life savings and organized an expedition. The expedition, based near Iquitos, Peru, took place in 2009 and lasted for 12 days.

During the expedition, Warner hired a local pilot, Jorge Pinedo, to fly over the area. Warner's son Greg sat up front with the pilot and took hundreds of photographs. Additionally, the plane was outfitted with two video cameras that constantly recorded the ground below. In all, five hours of video footage and over 700 still images were obtained. Analysis of the media revealed what appeared to be a large snake working its way through a channel.[15] The Warners shared their findings with the Peruvian government and with researchers from the National Geographic Society and Queens University in Belfast. Mike Warner's website www.bigsnakes.info contains much information and a series of videos outlining his research. A copy of the report from the expedition can also be downloaded.

The Moronococha Incident

A terrifying, yet remarkable event occurred in Moronococha, Peru in 2009, when a massive snake destroyed the home of Dolores Shuna. Her home was built on stilts and sat above the water. One evening, a large mass of vegetation, estimated to be about 200 square meters (2153 square feet) in size, was pushed into the home thereby destroying it. Afterward, the mass of vegetation returned to its original position.

Shuna and Don Manuel, her husband, saw the mass move toward the home, but did not see the body of snake. Shuna caught a glimpse of the snake's head, which was black and about 2 meters wide (6.5 feet). She compared the eyes of the serpent to the lights on a boat. The mass of debris moved over 100 feet to get to the house, and then pushed the house an incredible distance of about 200 feet. Don Artemio was nearby and helped the pair to safety. Artemio claimed the snake was dark in color and the size of a tree. Other witnesses who spotted the creature said that it had horns.[16]

This unimaginable incident was not the couple's first run-in with the gargantuan snake. Shuna is convinced that the snake wanted to get rid of them. She and her husband had noticed that the mass of vegetation had moved around before finally crashing into their home. However, during times of heavy wind, the island remained stationary. Could it be that the Yacumama was positioning this floating island to use later to attack the dwelling? The couple had also experienced loud bumping against the stilts of their home. On nights when the bumping occurred, the air was heavy with the smell of a reptile. The smell was described as being similar to the urination of a boa.[17]

As strange as it sounds for a large snake to push a "debris island" into a dwelling, this sort of thing has happened before. In 1930, Joao Penha claimed to see a Yacumama push a large pile of debris over 900 feet in the Río Iguape in Brazil. According to Penha, the snake had large, glowing eyes.

Another Awakening

In November 2009, at the settlement of AH Juan Pablo, on the outskirts of Iquitos, Peru, a Yacamama once again left a path of destruction when it came out of its deep sleep. The destruction was not nearly as drastic as the Nueva Tacna incident, but it is certainly worthy of mention.

For years, local residents believed that a giant boa was living beneath the ground. Oftentimes, tremors were felt; this was attributed to the giant boa moving or adjusting its position. Two residents, speaking in a documentary, claimed that years earlier they had seen a black boa come from the ground and tear a channel over 6 feet wide into the ground. It also broke a sidewalk and caused damage to the inside of a man's home. Similar to the Nueva Tacna incident, the creature cut a large channel through the ground as it headed toward a nearby swamp. Trees were uprooted and overturned at the entrance of the swamp.[18]

An Iquitos newspaper, *El Popular,* reported on the event. According to the report, residents heard sounds similar to those of a tractor, but were too frightened to investigate the loud noise. In the morning, locals were sure of what made the noise—a black boa. Evidence of the beast's presence was left in the form of a track 20 meters long and 5 meters wide (66 feet x 16 feet).

Sachamama

When several media outlets discussed the incidents mentioned earlier, they referred to the monster snake as the Sachamama. Many locals did as well. I believe that all of the names given to this animal, including the generic term "giant anaconda," are pointing to the same creature. However, the name Yacumama, "the mother of the water," and the name Sachamama, which means "jungle mother," may represent different phases in the snake's life.

According to Mike Warner, undoubtedly a subject matter expert, the Sachamama is an overgrown Yacumama that no longer uses the waterways, but is confined to land. Reptiles grow their entire lives, and many have surprisingly long lifespans. Imagine if a giant snake such as the Yacumama had a lifespan of 100 years, or even 50 years—as an apex predator, there is nothing to prevent it from reaching a truly extraordinary size. It stands to reason that as the behemoth grows, it eventually reaches the point where it becomes immobilized; it is then confined to the jungle—thus becoming the Sachamama, "mother of the jungle."

The giant snake's transition from predominantly being a water snake to a land snake makes sense and neatly fits various legends and folklore into one definable creature. The grounded giant lays on the jungle floor and the vegetation grows all around it. A person could walk into it without even knowing; and according to stories, people have. When the Sachamama dies, its body decomposes under the jungle canopy, its bones are swallowed up by the thick vegetation; evidence that the massive predator ever existed is wiped away. Like the lost cities of the Amazon—cities of gold—the enormity of the canopy and its impenetrable growth keep the secrets of the jungle well-hidden.

The dreaded Sachamama is most certainly a cannibal. Warner believes that the Sachamama, no longer able to hunt, releases pheromones to attract its own kind. When an unsuspecting Yacumama, seeking a mate, slithers close enough to the jungle mother, it is ambushed and devoured.[19] This hideous practice surely benefits mankind by keeping the population of the giants very low.

There are legends that state the Sachamama is able to use its eyes to put victims in a trance. This reminds me of Kaa, the snake from *The Jungle Book* who clumsily tries to hypnotize its prey. I wonder if this legend is misplaced; I think that perhaps it originated from the snake attracting other snakes through the release of pheromones—of course its eyes, large and phosphorescent, are the very thing of legends— maybe the eyes and the release of pheromones became intertwined in stories handed down for generations.

A Personal Story

Recently, I visited the Peruvian Amazon. In order to reach the eco lodge where I was staying, a lengthy, seemingly never-ending boat ride up the Río Tambopata was required. As the long and narrow boat fought its way upstream, through the occasional eddies, shallows, and obstructions, I became lost in my thoughts. The fact that I was on a boat heading into the Amazonian Rainforest was surreal; this dream of mine, which I had held onto for decades was unfolding before me. I was mesmerized by the jungle; I became lost in the vastness of this special place—and I was barely penetrating the Amazon—I was only safely skirting the outer edges of the mysterious jungle. Over and over, I thought to myself, *who knows what could be lurking in the dense, impenetrable rainforest; anything could be hidden here! It wouldn't surprise me at all if a real-life Jurassic Park was just beyond where I could see.*

The following night, while hiking through the jungle with only small flashlights to break up the indescribable darkness, I asked my guide, Chamo, about the Yacumama. Half expecting him to laugh at me, I began the conversation slowly. I started by asking a question that I already knew the answer to: "Are there anacondas here?" Chamo answered in the affirmative, and told me of an anaconda that he saw nearby about a year ago. He claimed that the snake was 9 meters in length (29.5 feet). Later on, I viewed some of his photographs of the snake—a truly impressive specimen.

After a little talk about anacondas, I pressed on, seeking answers to what I really wanted to know. I asked Chamo, "What about the Yacumama, or the giant anaconda, is there anything like that around here? Do you believe the Yacumama is real?" Through the flickering of a flashlight I could see his face tighten and grow serious. He replied, "Sí, yes it's real. I have not seen it, but I know it's real. My grandmother told me about it. She saw it."

To say I was ecstatic is an understatement—after years of researching the "water monster" phenomenon, I was face-to-face, speaking to a local with firsthand knowledge of the biggest monster of them all—the Yacumama!

Chamo went on, "She told me it was really big, and when it woke up—you know, they sleep a really long time—it shook the ground. It went in the river and that's when she saw it." He spoke more about the Yacumama, making it clear that the snake hibernates or sleeps—for many years. According to his story, the Yacumama entered the Río Madre de Dios where the Río Tambopota dumps into it. This account is consistent with the research of Mike Warner; Warner often stresses that the Yacumama prefers the confluence of two rivers. I told Chamo that I had heard and read that areas where rivers meet are favorable to the Yacumama. He nodded his head in agreement.

Moments later, Chamo shook his head and said, "It is real, I believe the Yacumama is real." I was giddy with excitement after listening to Chamo's story. As soon as I was able, I wrote down what I had heard in a small notebook I carry.

The next day, Chamo spoke again about the Yacumama. He said, "When it woke up, the river went like this." He made a shaking motion with his hands. Incredibly, the Río Madre de Dios shook and moved when the giant came out of its lengthy slumber.

Chamo expressed some trepidation that the city of Puerto Maldonado, which is densely populated with about 75,000 residents, could experience devastation when the Yacumama wakes up again. Given the instances covered earlier, this fear is reasonable—Puerto Maldonado has a denser population than the other areas that have experienced destruction at the hands of the Yacumama. If by chance a Yacumama is living beneath Puerto Maldonado, many homes and critical infrastructure could be destroyed the next time the snake makes its way to the river. Maybe though, this fear is misplaced. Remembering back to the Nueva Tacna incident, after the snake entered the river, it relocated to the next confluence. Perhaps the Yacumama that Chamo's grandmother saw did the same.

I, of all people, understand that the story I recounted is purely anecdotal; it offers nothing to prove the existence of the Yacumama.

Even if Chamo had seen the snake himself, skeptics would blame seismic activity and or misidentification. Perhaps the naysayers are correct. However, I am undeterred—I believe. I agree with Chamo when he said, "The jungle is alive. It has secrets, we don't know what happens inside it. We don't know everything about it."

The Minhocão

The Minhocão is a giant, burrowing creature whose name means "giant earthworm" in Portuguese. Tales of the Minhocão were widely reported during the 1800s, and native legends go back for centuries. However, by the 20th century, the creature seemed to have become inactive or gone extinct. That is unless, as I believe, that the Minhocão is actually the same creature as the Yacumama.

The physical appearance of the Minhocão is described as being very similar to the Yacumama. It is black in color and reaches a length of 150 feet and a width of up to 15 feet. It is covered with an armor-like hide, and has horns on its head.

Like the Yacumama, the Minhocão is known for its burrowing. This behavior is quite destructive. Trees are uprooted; river channels are created; large trenches are cut into the landscape; roads are collapsed and destroyed; homes are often damaged as well. Both the Minhocão and Yacumama are blamed for causing tremors with their underground movements. It is frightening to think of an underground creature large enough to mimic seismic activity! The 1990 Science Fiction film *Tremors* comes to mind. Perhaps both the Minhocão and Yacumama can claim a connection to Kevin Bacon when playing the game "Six Degrees of Kevin Bacon."

A New Underground Monster

The scientific journal *Nature* published a report on the enormous *earthworm* on February 21, 1878. The article appeared in pages 325–326 and was titled "A New Underground Monster." The entire article is reprinted below:

> A recent communication from Fritz Müller, of Itajahy, in Southern Brazil, to the Zoologische Garten contains a wonderful account of the supposed existence of a gigantic earthworm in the highlands of the southern provinces of Brazil, where it is known as the "Minhocão." The stories told of this supposed animal, says Fritz Müller, sound for the most part so

incredible, that one is tempted to consider them as fabulous. Who could repress a smile at hearing men speak of a worm some fifty yards in length, and five in breadth, covered with bones as with a coat of armour, uprooting mighty pine trees as if they were blades of grass, diverting the courses of streams into fresh channels, and turning dry land into a bottomless morass? And yet after carefully considering the different accounts given of the "Minhocao," one can hardly refuse to believe that some such animal does really exist, although not quite so large as the country folk would have us to believe.

About eight years ago a "Minhocão" appeared in the neighbourhood of Lages. Francisco de Amaral Varella, when about ten kilometres distant from that town, saw lying on the bank of the Rio das Caveiras a strange animal of gigantic size, nearly one metre in thickness, not very long, and with a snout like a pig, but whether it had legs or not he could not tell. He did not dare to seize it alone, and whilst calling his neighbours to his assistance, it vanished, not without leaving palpable marks behind it in the shape of a trench as it disappeared under the earth. A week later a similar trench, perhaps constructed by the same animal, was seen on the opposite side of Lages, about six kilometres distant from the former, and the traces were followed', which led ultimately under the roots of a large pine tree, and were lost in the marshy land. Herr F. Kelling, from whom this information was obtained, was at that time living as a merchant in Lages, and saw himself the trenches made by the "Minhocão." Herr E. Odebrecht, while surveying a line of road from Ita jahy into the highlands of the province of Santa Caterina, several years ago, crossed a broad marshy plain traversed by an arm of the river Marombas. His progress here was much impeded by devious winding trenches which followed the course of the stream, and occasionally lost themselves in it. At the time Herr Odebrecht could not understand the origin of these peculiar trenches, but is now inclined to believe that they were the work of the "Minhocão."

About fourteen years ago, in the month of January, Antonio José Branco, having been absent with his whole family eight days from his house, which was situated on one of the tributaries of the Rio dos Cachorros, ten kilometres from Curitibanos, on returning home found the road undermined, heaps of earth being thrown up, and large trenches made. These trenches commenced at the source of a brook, and followed its windings; terminating ultimately in a morass after a course of from 700 to 1,000 metres. The breadth of the trenches was said to be about three metres. Since that period the brook has flowed in the trench made by the "Minhocão." The path of the animal lay generally beneath the surface of the earth under the bed of the stream; several pine trees had been rooted up by its passage. One of the trees from which the "Minhocão" in passing had torn off the bark and part of the wood, was said to be still standing and visible last year. Hundreds of people from Curitibanos and other places had come to see the devastation caused by the "Minhocão," and supposed the animal to be still living in the marshy pool, the waters of which appeared at certain times to be suddenly and strangely troubled. Indeed on still nights a rumbling sound like distant thunder and a slight movement of the earth was sensible in the neighbouring dwellings. This story was told to Herr Müller by two eye-witnesses, Jose", son of old Branco, and a stepson, who formerly lived in the same house. Herr Müller remarks that the appearance of the "Minhocão" is always supposed to presage a period of rainy weather.

In the neighbourhood of the Rio dos Papagaios, in the province of Parana, one evening in 1849 after a long course of rainy weather, a sound was heard in the house of a certain Joao de Deos, as if rain were again falling in a wood hard by, but on looking out, the heavens were seen to be bright with stars. On the following morning it was discovered that a large piece of land on the further side of a small hill had been entirely undermined, and was traversed by deep trenches which led towards a bare open plateau covered with stones, or what is called in this district a "legeado." At this spot large heaps of clay turned up out of the earth marked the onward course of the animal from the legeado into the bed of a stream running into the Papagaios. Three years after this place was visited by Senhor Lebino José dos Santos, a wealthy proprietor, now resident near Curitibanos. He saw the ground still upturned, the mounds of clay on the rocky plateau, and the remains of the moved earth in the rocky bed of the brook quite plainly, and came to the conclusion that it must have been the work of two animals, the size of which must have been from two to three metres in breadth.

In the same neighbourhood, according to Senhor Lebino, a "Minhocão" had been seen several times before. A black woman going to draw water from a pool near a house one morning, according to her usual practice, found the whole pool destroyed, and saw a short distance off an animal which she described as being as big as a house moving off along the ground. The people whom she summoned to see the monster were too late, and found only traces of the animal, which had apparently plunged over a neighbouring cliff into deep water. In the same district a young man saw a huge pine suddenly overturned, when there was no wind and no one to cut it. On hastening up to discover the cause, he found the surrounding earth in movement, and an enormous worm like black animal in the middle of it, about twenty-five metres long, and with two horns on its head.

In the province of Sao Paulo, as Senhor Lebino also states, not far from Ypanema, is a spot that is still called Charquinho, that is, Little

Marsh, as it formerly was, but some years ago a "Minhocão" made a trench through the marsh into the Ypanema River, and so converted it into the bed of a stream.

In the year 1849, Senhor Lebino was on a journey near Arapehy, in the State of Uruguay. There he was told that there was a dead "Minhocão" to be seen a few miles off, which had got wedged into a narrow cleft of a rock, and so perished. Its skin was said to be as thick as the bark of a pine-tree, and formed of hard scales like those of an armadillo.

From all these stories it would appear conclusive that in the high district where the Uruguay and the Parana have their sources, excavations, and long trenches are met with, which are undoubtedly the work of some living animal. Generally, if not always, they appear after continued rainy weather, and seem to start from marshes or river-beds, and to enter them again. The accounts as to the size and appearance of the creature are very uncertain. It might be suspected to be a gigantic fish allied to Lepidosircn and Ceratodus; the "swine's snout," would show some resemblance to Ceratodus, while the horns on the body rather point to the front limbs of Lepidosiren, if these particulars can be at all depended upon. In any case, concludes Herr Müller, it would be worthwhile to make further investigations about the "Minhocão," and, if possible, to capture it for a zoological garden!

To conclude this remarkable story, we may venture to suggest whether, if any such animal really exist, which, upon the testimony produced by Fritz Müller, appears very probable, it may not rather be a relic of the rare of gigantic armadilloes which in past geological epochs were so abundant in Southern Brazil. The little Chlamydo- phorus truncatus is, we believe, mainly, if not entirely, subterranean in its habits. May there not still exist a larger representative of the same or nearly allied genus, or, if the suggestion be not too bold, even a last descendant of the Glyptodonts?

Closing Thoughts

In light of the anecdotal evidence—of which there is an abundance—it certainly seems that *something* strange has been going on in South America for centuries. Moreover, it seems that whatever is causing damage is enormous in size and truly terrifying.

It also seems clear that the Minhocão and Yacumama are one in the same—the same frightening beast that gouges trenches into the earth as it makes its way toward the water. Dr. Karl Shuker has suggested that the Minhocão might be an enormous caecilian, a burrowing amphibian. Mike Warner has also suggested that the Yacumama might be a caecilian.

I do not know what to make of the Minhocão, Yacumama, or "giant anaconda"—other than to say, if they exist, more likely than not they are of the same species. Whatever species that may be. If this monster exists, and I believe that it probably does, it is an absolutely terrifying thought. This creature is horrible—a true monster in every sense of the word.

"The horror! The horror!"
— Joseph Conrad, *Heart of Darkness*

Living Dinosaurs?

[15] Behold now behemoth, which I made with thee; he eateth grass as an ox.[16] Lo now, his strength is in his loins, and his force is in the navel of his belly.[17] He moveth his tail like a cedar: the sinews of his stones are wrapped together.[18] His bones are as strong pieces of brass; his bones are like bars of iron.[19] He is the chief of the ways of God: he that made him can make his sword to approach unto him.[20] Surely the mountains bring him forth food, where all the beasts of the field play.[21] He lieth under the shady trees, in the covert of the reed, and fens.[22] The shady trees cover him with their shadow; the willows of the brook compass him about.[23] Behold, he drinketh up a river, and hasteth not: he trusteth that he can draw up Jordan into his mouth.[24] He taketh it with his eyes: his nose pierceth through snares.
—Job 40:15-24 (King James Version)

This question may sound ridiculous, yet in my mind, it is worth asking: Could there be creatures alive today that are thought to be extinct? More specifically, could there somehow be dinosaurs alive today? If so, the South American continent is certainly home to some of them, particularly the vast, virtually untouched regions of the Amazon Rainforest. As outlandish as it may sound to suggest that there could be modern-day dinosaurs roaming the Amazon, the notion may not be quite so crazy.

From the earliest days of European exploration of South America, reports of strange, dinosaur-like creatures have emerged.

One of the most intriguing reports of dinosaurs in South America comes from Bolivia. The account was published in the *Scientific American* in 1883. The article is titled, "A Bolivian Saurian." An excerpt is printed below:

"The Brazilian Minister at La Paz, Bolivia, has remitted to the Minister of Foreign Affairs in Rio photographs of drawings of an extraordinary saurian killed on the Beni after receiving thirty-six balls. By order of the President of Bolivia the dried body, which had been preserved in Asuncion, was sent to La Paz. It is twelve meters long from snout to point of the tail, which latter is flattened. Besides the anterior head, it has, four meters behind, two small but completely formed heads rising from the back. All three have much resemblance to the head of a dog. The legs are short, and end in formidable claws. The legs, belly, and lower part of the throat appear defended by a kind of scale armor, and all the back is protected by a still thicker and double cuirass, starting from behind the ears of the anterior head, and continuing to the tail. The neck is long, and the belly large and almost dragging on the ground. Professor Gilveti, who examined the beast, thinks it is not a monster, but a member of a rare or almost lost species, as the Indians in some parts of Bolivia use small earthen vases of identical shape, and probably copied from nature." Mr. William E. A. Axon, in a note giving the above to the Journal of Science, says: "If this account should prove to be accurate, it would form a counterpart to the etching of the mammoth, which forms so interesting a memorial of prehistoric art."

Renowned adventurer Percy Fawcett explored the jungles of South America extensively. During the height of the rubber trade, he was hired by the Royal Geographical Society to survey highly disputed boundaries in the remote jungle along the border of Bolivia and Brazil. He is probably remembered most, though, for his, along with his son's, disappearance. The pair went missing while searching for the lost city of "Z."

During Fawcett's expeditions into jungle, he claimed to have encountered many unusual creatures. The most unusual by far, was a creature that some believe may have been a diplodocus—a large sauropod dinosaur. Fawcett gave this account in the *Daily Mail* in 1919:

"A friend of mine, a trader in the rivers and for whose honesty I can vouch, saw in somewhere about Latitude 12 South and Longitude 65 West the head and neck of a huge reptile of the character of the brontosaurus…The savages appear to be familiar with the existence and tracks of the beast, although I have never come across any of the latter myself."

In the same article, Fawcett also pointed out something very important when considering the existence of dinosaurs in South America. He said:

"These swamps over immense areas are **virtually impenetrable**." (Emphasis added.)

Recorded in the book, *Exploration Fawcett,* is a passage written by Fawcett, in which he described a strange animal:

"There are snakes and insects unknown to scientists, and in the forests of the Madidi some mysterious and enormous beast has frequently been disturbed in the swamps—possibly a primeval monster like those reported in other parts of the continent. Certainly, tracks have been found belonging to no known animal—huge tracks, far greater than could have been made by any species we know."

Figure 4: The renowned explorer Percy Fawcett.

Fawcett was not the only explorer that told of dinosaur-like creatures in the remote forests of South America. Renowned explorer and former OSS Agent, Leonard Clark (1908–1957), became familiar with tales from indigenous tribes of large, long-necked reptiles that would attack canoes when approached. According to the natives, the creatures fed on vegetation, and their descriptions of the animals were consistent with that of a dinosaur similar to the diplodocus.

Reported Sightings

There is a plethora of reported dinosaur sightings from South America over the last 150 years. The reports are fairly consistent; large reptilian creatures, similar in nature to sauropod dinosaurs, are known to the indigenous people and have been spotted by others as well.

A creature, that could best be described as an aquatic dinosaur was seen in a swampy region of Peru in 1907. Franz Herrmann Schmidt and Rudolf Phleng saw a creature about 35 feet in length with flippers and a snake-like head. The pair shot at the animal, but gunfire apparently had little to no effect on the animal.[1]

During Schmidt and Phleng's expedition, they discovered floating islands with large wallows. Could this have been the same "debris islands" that have reportedly been pushed about by the Yacaumama?

In 1921, there were reports of a dinosaur-like creature in Columbia's Río Magdalena. Similarly, in Argentina during the 1930's, a possible dinosaur was spotted in Lago Pellegrini on several occasions.

Silvano Lorenzoni wrote a couple of articles in the late 1970s about reports of dinosaur-like creatures in Venezuela. He mentioned large reptiles similar to lizards being spotted in the mountain valleys near the coast.[2]

In 1931, Swedish explorer, Harald Westin, saw a creature about 20 feet long on the banks of the Río Mamoré, along the border of Brazil and Bolivia. The animal had four legs and a body similar to a boa constrictor.[3] I wonder about this account. Should this report be classified as a possible dinosaur sighting? Judging only from the brief description, the animal sounds similar to an alligator or crocodile. As with many cryptid sightings, details are lacking. This is not surprising, though, as typical encounters tend to be very brief.

An unusual account comes from Alexander Laime, who saw three plesiosaur-like creatures in 1955. The animals were lying on a river bank in Venezuela. Strangely, each creature was only about three feet long, yet they looked similar to a plesiosaur.[4] Obviously, if there are dinosaurs alive today, there has to be small, breeding populations. It might sound crazy to ask, but did Laime see a group of juvenile plesiosaurs? Or, did he see some entirely different? Or, is the whole story just a bunch of nonsense?

In 1975, river guide Sebastian Bastos told a Swiss businessman about dinosaur-like creatures that were well-known to the indigenous people of the area. The natives tried their best to avoid the monstrous creatures, and had tales of canoes being flipped over by the aggressive beasts. The dinosaurs were over 18 feet in length and would occasionally come onto shore at night. Bastos claimed to have survived an attack by the creatures.[5]

Two large saurian creatures, estimated to be 30 feet long, were observed by a group of geology students in 1995. The students were studying quartz deposits in Brazil's Sincora Mountains when they saw the creatures in the shallows of the Río Paraguaçu.[6] Some may think that this report is false; after all, it would not be unusual for students to pull a prank. However, I do not believe it is reasonable to assume that a group of students would just make this story up. Wouldn't a story like this bring ridicule to the students, the university, and their program? Ultimately, wouldn't fabricating this story risk devaluing their degrees and education? Of course, the story cannot be corroborated; it also cannot be disproven. Sound familiar?

An Eye-opener

On a recent trip to Peru, while browsing through a section of pre-Inca pottery in the Larco Museum in Lima, something grabbed my attention and stopped me in my tracks. I couldn't believe what I was seeing; it looked as if a pre-Inca civilization had created a depiction of a dinosaur out of clay.

Figure 5: This looks like a dinosaur to me; of course, interpretations may vary! Photo taken by the author.

I was excited with my "find;" I snapped several photographs and began searching the room for anything else that resembled a dinosaur. I was unable to locate any other pottery that reminded me of dinosaurs; I was on a tight schedule and could not devote the time that I needed to thoroughly search the pottery room. Still, though, I could not have been happier with my "discovery."

Of course, upon further examination of the artifact, it quickly became apparent that it been stylized and artistic liberties had been taken. The animal has a hand that appears to be holding an arrow or some sort of weapon. It would be easy for a debunker to say that the creature is mythical; the fact that it appears to be holding a weapon only bolsters their claim.

Figure 6: Photo taken by the author.

The fact that the reptile has been artistically enhanced does not sway my opinion; the piece passes "the eye test." When I first saw the artifact, I immediately thought—***dinosaur!*** Consider this: many animals are depicted in paintings and sculptures which display human-like characteristics. This in and of itself does not make the creature mythical—the animal is based on something real. Take the obverse of the Great Seal of the United States for instance—an eagle cannot hold clusters of arrows in one talon, an olive branch in the other, while carrying a scroll with its beak. Despite the fancy stylization of the eagle on the Great Seal, it goes without saying that eagles exist; they are not mythical.

Figure 7: The Obverse of the Great Seal of the United States.

What Should We Think?

Is it possible? Can it be? Are there living dinosaurs in South America 65 million years after they were supposed to have gone extinct? I understand that hard evidence is lacking; yet, can there be any doubt that *something* strange is being observed?

Perhaps it would be easier to dismiss the accounts mentioned here if the phenomenon was limited to South America—but it isn't. Reports of dinosaur-like creatures come from Papua New Guinea, Africa, and Asia. It could be argued that dragons, embedded in the folklore of cultures all over the world, are in reality modern-day dinosaurs.

Although this book is dedicated to water monsters "South of the Border," it is difficult to imagine concluding this discussion of modern-day dinosaurs without devoting some time to the most famous living dinosaur of them all—Mokele-mbembe, a dinosaur-like creature that lives in the most remote reaches of the Congo.

Mokele-mbembe

I was first introduced to the Congolese modern-day dinosaur, Mokele-mbembe, in the 1990s through a series of "creation seminars" that had been recorded on VHS tapes. The presenter was Dr. Kent Hovind, also known as "Dr. Dino." Hovind is a biblical creationist of the "Young Earth" school of thought. Young Earth Creationists believe that God created the earth in six literal 24 hour-days; and, based on biblical genealogies, the earth is about 6,000 years old. Being that the planet is so young, creationists believe that dinosaurs and man lived side-by-side; they were contemporaries. Moreover, according to the Young Earth Creationism (YEC) model, some dinosaurs are alive today.

The Old Testament passage that I opened this section with is often used by YEC enthusiasts when discussing dinosaurs. According to their reasoning, these verses are a clear reference to dinosaurs. In the passage, God is speaking to his servant Job about one of the masterpieces and wonders of his creation. Many YEC proponents believe that God is speaking of none other than the Apatosaurus.

There is another biblical passage that some believe refers to a dinosaur. It also comes from the book of Job:

> Canst thou draw out leviathan with an hook? or his tongue with a cord which thou lettest down? [2] Canst thou put an hook into his nose? or bore his jaw through with a thorn? [3] Will he make many supplications unto thee? will he speak soft words unto thee? [4] Will he make a covenant with thee? wilt thou take him for a servant for ever? [5] Wilt thou play with him as with a bird? or wilt thou bind him for thy maidens? [6] Shall the companions make a banquet of him? shall they part him among the merchants? [7] Canst thou fill his skin with barbed irons? or his head with fish spears? [8] Lay thine hand upon him, remember the battle, do no more. [9] Behold, the hope of him is in vain: shall not one be cast down even at the sight of him? [10] None is so fierce that dare stir him up: who then is able to stand before me? [11] Who hath prevented me, that I should repay him? whatsoever is under the whole heaven is mine. [12] I will not conceal his parts, nor his power, nor his comely proportion. [13] Who can discover

the face of his garment? or who can come to him with his double bridle? [14] Who can open the doors of his face? his teeth are terrible round about. [15] His scales are his pride, shut up together as with a close seal. [16] One is so near to another, that no air can come between them. [17] They are joined one to another, they stick together, that they cannot be sundered. [18] By his neesings a light doth shine, and his eyes are like the eyelids of the morning. [19] Out of his mouth go burning lamps, and sparks of fire leap out. [20] Out of his nostrils goeth smoke, as out of a seething pot or caldron. [21] His breath kindleth coals, and a flame goeth out of his mouth. [22] In his neck remaineth strength, and sorrow is turned into joy before him. [23] The flakes of his flesh are joined together: they are firm in themselves; they cannot be moved. [24] His heart is as firm as a stone; yea, as hard as a piece of the nether millstone. [25] When he raiseth up himself, the mighty are afraid: by reason of breakings they purify themselves. [26] The sword of him that layeth at him cannot hold: the spear, the dart, nor the habergeon. [27] He esteemeth iron as straw, and brass as rotten wood. [28] The arrow cannot make him flee: slingstones are turned with him into stubble. [29] Darts are counted as stubble: he laugheth at the shaking of a spear. [30] Sharp stones are under him: he spreadeth sharp pointed things upon the mire. [31] He maketh the deep to boil like a pot: he maketh the sea like a pot of ointment. [32] He maketh a path to shine after him; one would think the deep to be hoary. [33] Upon earth there is not his like, who is made without fear. [34] He beholdeth all high things: he is a king over all the children of pride.

—Job 41 (King James Version)

Are the Young Earth Creationists correct? Does the Bible mention dinosaurs? You be the judge. Personally, I'm not sure what to make of the verses. I'm not convinced that dinosaurs are being discussed; I also do not rule out the possibility. I do find the verses very intriguing and I always have.

Before going any further, allow me to state that *I do not share the views of Young Earth Creationists.* In fact, I am not religious at all—I don't even bother attending organized religious services at Christmas or Easter. With that being said, though, I owe a great deal to Young Earth Creationists such as Dr. Kent Hovind. Hovind's seminars introduced me to several cryptids that I had never heard of, and helped to open my mind to the idea of living dinosaurs. This greatly furthered my passion for cryptozoology. Beyond that, Young Earth Creationists have done a lot of good field work and research which has benefited the field of cryptozoology.

Now that I have ran down a rabbit hole of Young Earth Creationism and the Book of Job, it is time to steer the conversation back to the matter at hand. So without further hesitation, let's get back to our living dinosaur, Mokele-mbembe.

There have been reports of a massive creature in the African Congo since the late 1700s when French missionaries discovered enormous tracks. In 1776, the abbot Lievain Bonaventure Proyart, wrote about the tracks in the *History of Loango, Kakonga, and other Kingdoms in Africa*. The following is an excerpt from an English translation published in 1914:

> It must be monstrous, the prints of its claws are seen upon the earth, and formed an impression on it of about three feet in circumference. In observing the posture and disposition of the footprints, they concluded that it did not run this part of the way, and that it carried its claws at a distance of seven or eight feet one from the other.[7]

During the early 1900s, present-day Cameroon was a German colony. Captain Freiherr von Stein zu Lausnitz made mention of a strange creature known by the locals as Mokele-mbembe after conducting a survey of the region:

> The animal is said to be of a brownish gray color . . . its size approximating that of an elephant. It is said to have a long and very flexible neck. Some spoke of a long muscular tail like that of an alligator. Canoes coming near it are said to be doomed; the animals are said to attack the vessels at once and to kill the crews but without eating the bodies. The creature is said to live in the caves that have been washed out by the river in the clay of its shores at sharp bends. It is said to climb the shore even in daytime in search of its food; its diet is said to be entirely vegetable.[8]

It is obvious from the early reports that *something* strange, and something to be feared was roaming the remote reaches of the Congo.

There have been at least 50 expeditions to the region.[9] It was an expedition in the late 1970s, though, that brought tales of Mokele-mbembe to the forefront.

Herpetologist James Powell travelled to Gabon in 1976 to study crocodiles. During his time there, he began to amass a number of reports of a large river monster. A local witchdoctor identified the monster as a diplodocus when flipping through Powell's book of dinosaurs. Upon Powell's return to the United States, he shared his experiences with cryptozoologist Roy P. Mackal (1925–2013). Mackal accompanied Powell on a trip to the People's Republic of the Congo in 1979 to investigate the matter in person. Numerous eyewitnesses shared their stories with Mackal, and identified the diplodocus as Mokele-mbembe when looking through his book of dinosaurs.[10]

Beginning his quest in the 1980s, Young Earth Creationist William J. Gibbons has been on several expeditions to the Congo in search of Mkole-mbembe. Like Mackal and Powell, Gibbons heard many stories of encounters with the dinosaur from eyewitnesses. During Gibbons' visits with local villagers, he was told of other dinosaurs which inhabit the area as well. Writing for the Institute for Creation Research's magazine *Impact* in the July 2002 issue, he said the following:

> Additional information was also gathered about other strange animals that reputedly inhabit the forest and swamps, including a large quadruped armed with a heavy neck frill and up to four horns on its head. Our witnesses immediately picked out a picture of the triceratops as being a dead ringer for this animal which is reputed to kill and disembowel elephants.

Recently, Gibbons was fundraising for another expedition to the Congo to search for Mokele-mbembe. Originally the expedition was set for 2015; as of this writing, he had not raised the necessary funds.[11]

Many books have been written about Mokele-mbembe, and the creature was even featured on one of History's *MonsterQuest* episodes. Internet rumors have swirled as of late of the death of a Mokele-mbembe, supposedly shot by Pygmies. There were similar tales in 1960, when Pygmy villagers allegedly speared a Mokele-mbembe to death.[12]

The Ica Stones

No discussion of South American dinosaurs could ever be complete without at least briefly discussing the Ica Stones. The Ica Stones, from the Ica region of Peru, are highly controversial; dismissed as hoaxes by naysayers, these andesite stones are engraved with pictures of dinosaurs and scenes depicting advanced technology. Several recognizable species of dinosaurs such as the diplodocus and triceratops are engraved on various stones. Other stones show heart surgery being performed and what appears to be people looking through a large telescope. The stones, and the scenes, are too numerous to mention here; these are but a few examples.

Figure 8: One of the Ica Stones. Dinosaurs are clearly depicted. By Brattarb (Own work) [CC BY-SA 3.0 (http://creativecommons.org/licenses/by-sa/3.0) or GFDL (http://www.gnu.org/copyleft/fdl.html)], via Wikimedia Commons. https://commons.wikimedia.org/wiki/File:Ica_stones3.JPG

Contrary to what many skeptics claim—that the stones are modern forgeries—the first mention of the Ica Stones occurred during the Spanish conquest of the Inca Empire. In 1535, a Jesuit priest recorded that he had viewed the stones, and was astonished.[13]

No one has done more to present the enigmatic stones to the world than Dr. Javier Cabrera. Cabrera introduced the world to the perplexing Ica Stones after receiving a stone as a birthday present in 1966. Cabrera recognized that a species of fish, which had gone extinct millions of years ago, was depicted on the stone. Cabrera was intrigued by what was portrayed; word of this quickly spread to the Soldi brothers, who were collectors of artifacts that predated the Incas. The brothers showed Cabrera thousands of similar stones they had in their possession. According to the brothers, archaeologists had shown little-to-no interest in the artifacts. Cabrera, however, was extremely interested; he purchased 341 Ica Stones from the Soldi brothers for a price equivalent to about 45 American dollars.[14]

In addition to the brothers, Cabrera found other sources and continued collecting the stones. He started a museum to house the Ica Stones, and by the 1970s, he had amassed over 11,000.

Trouble began for Cabrera—and the Ica Stones for that matter—after a BBC documentary brought the attention of the Peruvian government to the matter. Cabrera's source for most of the stones, Basilio Uschuya, was arrested under an antiquities law for selling the stones. After his arrest, Uschuya claimed that the artifacts were fake—he had carved the andesite stones himself.

There's no way to know for sure, but Uschuya's admission may have been been false—and self-serving. According to many who believe in the authenticity of the Ica Stones, Uschuya may have admitted to carving the stones to escape prosecution for selling artifacts. You see, if he admitted to forging the stones, the consequences would be far less severe than if he had been selling pre-Inca artifacts.

At any rate, the Peruvian government concluded that the Ica Stones were nothing more than a hoax.[15] Case closed. Or was it?

Cabrera was not deterred by the admission of Uschuya. He devoted his life to defending the authenticity of the Ica Stones. Cabrera believed that the number of the stones, over 15,000, proved that they could not have been faked. Even if Uschuya carved the stones himself, he would have had to produce one stone a day for over 40 years to meet to volume in existence.[16] This is a tall order even if an entire team of hoaxers were involved.

Today, the Ica Stones have largely been dismissed as frauds. However, it should be pointed out that another possibility exists—what if some of the stones are forged, while others are genuine? Stones cannot be dated with any certainty due to a lack of organic material. Also, the mention of the stones by a Jesuit in the sixteenth century certainly lends credibility to the idea of the authenticity of at least some of the stones. Moreover, Cabrera's father had a similar collection that he amassed in the 1930s—long before Uschuya's forgery claims.

Those who believe in the possibility of living dinosaurs will be encouraged by pre-Incan artifacts depicting dinosaurs—naysayers will scoff at the idea. And so it goes.

Figure 9: Pre-Inca pottery from Peru. Is the figure on the vase a depiction of a dinosaur? Copyright Don Patton. www.bible.ca/tracks. Used with permission.

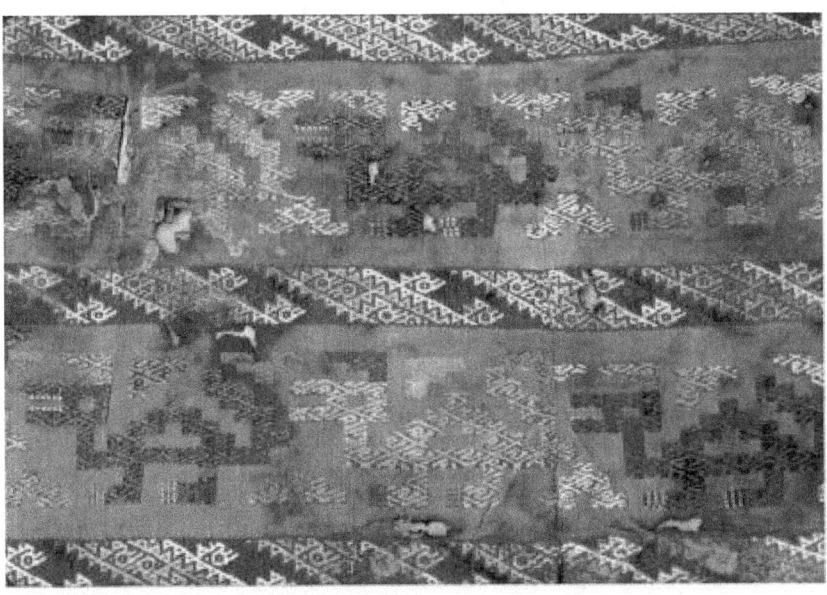

Figure 10: Are dinosaurs being depicted on this pre-Inca blanket? Copyright Don Patton. www.bible.ca/tracks. Used with permission.

The Patagonian Plesiosaur

The Patagonia region of Argentina is home to a creature whose description closely resembles that of a plesiosaur—a large marine reptile from the Mesozoic Era. Dubbed "Nahuelito" by the locals, aptly named after Lago Nahuel Huapi—the lake in which it dwells; reports of this strange animal have been occurring since the early 1900s and perhaps much earlier.

Patagonia, much like Canada and the northern United States, has a landscape that is dotted with glacial lakes. It is in these deep, icy waters that aquatic cryptids—similar to the quintessential lake monsters of North America—are said to dwell. In my first book I asked, and now I ask the question again: *Why do glacial lakes consistently produce rumors of large, prehistoric creatures?* Glacial lakes and cryptids go hand in hand; there is a definite correlation.

The waters of Lago Nahuel Huapi cover over 200 square miles. The lake reaches a maximum depth of over 1400 feet, and has a mean depth of over 500 feet. If an animal such as a modern-day plesiosaur exists, then it is a sure bet that Lake Nahuel Huapi provides a prime habitat for the creature.

Sightings

The Patagonian Plesiosaur came to prominence in the early 1920s. A decade before its fame, Canadian George Garrett and his son saw the creature while sailing on Lake Nahuel Huapi. Garrett gave his account to the *Toronto Globe* who reported the story in 1922. Garrett claimed that many of the local Indians knew of the creature and spoke of "immense water animals." Shortly after Garrett's encounter, two British prospectors also saw the animal.

It was the American prospector Martin Sheffield who did the most to bring attention to the Nahuelito. In 1922, he wrote to Dr. Clementi Onelli, director of the Buenos Aires Zoo, and told him about an encounter that he had with the Nahuelito. Sheffield noted that the creature had a long, swan-like neck and a large, rounded body. Onelli had been receiving similar reports, albeit sporadically, since the late 1890s.[1]

After Sheffield's correspondence, Onelli decided that it was time to conduct a field investigation. Onelli headed up an expedition to Lake Nahuel Huapi led by José Cihagi, the superintendent of the Buenos Aires Zoo. The operation was unsuccessful; nothing definitive came from it. As a result, the *Scientific American* reported that if a plesiosaur ever did exist in the lake, it certainly wasn't there any longer.

In February of 1978, on a day in which the lake was still and calm, a lady referred to as Señora Rumboll saw a long-necked animal. Several other people were also present during the sighting. According to the report, the creature's neck was about nine feet in length. Some of the eyewitnesses believed that what they saw may have actually been the periscope of a submarine.[2]

Figure 11: Artist's interpretation of a plesiosaur.

Periscopes? Submarines? As strange is this may sound in a lake, it is not entirely without precedent. Submarines have been mistaken for sea monsters off of the coast of Argentina, especially during the Cold War. Of course, it is a monumental stretch to insinuate that spy submarines off the coast are somehow related to happenings in a Patagonian lake. However, the thought of submarines in a lake brings to mind a creature that I wrote about in my first book. The creature is called Paddler, an Idaho lake monster thought by many to not be a monster at all, but rather, the product of the naval research and testing. The United States Navy's Acoustic Research Detachment, at Lake Pend Oreille, performs research on large-scale model submarines. Could something similar be going on in Lago Nueuel Huapi? If so, the powers that be are keeping a tight lid on it.

Jessica Campbell and several others saw the Nahuelito, or at least a multi-humped creature, on January 1, 1994. Incredibly, Campbell saw the creature again two years later. More incredible than that—she saw it twice on the same day! At one point, the animal swam past her as she was sitting on some rocks. Campbell recalled that when the creature was nearby, she could hear it breathing.[3]

Paula Jacarbe is another witness who claims to have heard the animal breathe. According to Jacarbe, the sound the creature makes when it breathes is very distinctive.[4]

Closing Thoughts

It is worth mentioning that other Patagonian lakes have had reports of similar creatures in their waters. Among these, is Lago Lácar. Lake Lácar is also a deep glacial lake. Perhaps unsurprisingly, it experienced a number of sightings during the 1950s. However, very few recent sightings have been reported. Lago Lácar is home to another creature, "El Cuero," which will be discussed in subsequent pages.

The Bío Bío River in Chile has also had its share of reports of a plesiosaur-like creature. The animal there has been known to leave tracks on the bank.

There have been sightings of creatures that match the Patagonian Pleasiosaur in Lake Llanquihue, Lake Todos los Santos, and Lake Esquel. There have also been sightings in the sea. In the early 1900s, a sighting occurred in the Strait of Magellan.

What is Nahuelito? A plesiosaur? A submarine? Something even more outlandish? Writing for the *Argentina Independent*, Sam Mustafa penned the following:

"The unknown always invites conspiracy. Some believe that Nahuelito is a mutant product of nuclear testing gone awry during the 1950s when Perón invited Nazi scientists to Argentina to compete with Russia and the USA in their arms race. In this Cold War context, Nahuelito was magnified by the sensationalism of the 1950s when the world was captivated by UFO sightings in Roswell and other such phenomenon."

Mustafa is correct; the unexplained does breed wild and bizarre theories. And why not? We are hard-wired to seek explanations. In the absence of definitive answers, everything is seemingly up for grabs. As for me, though, I don't subscribe to the mutant hypothesis or even the submarine explanation. Instead, I think that the Nahuelito is probably something similar to other lake monsters such as the Loch Ness Monster, the Ogopogo, and Champ. Whatever they are...

Cabralito

Unique video footage of a strange creature was captured on Christmas Day, 2011 in Argentina's Salta Province. The video was obtained by a fisherman in a manmade lake called Cabra Corral while he was filming lake scenery. When local news media outlets learned of the video, they quickly dubbed the animal "Cabralito"—this is a reference to the "Patagonian Plesiosaur," also known as Nahuelito, whose name references Nahuel Huapi, the lake where it resides.

Sebastian Papetti is the fisherman who obtained the video. He claimed that something strange in the water caught his eye as he was filming. What caught his attention was a creature—a creature that had a large wake following it, and was reptilian in appearance. The animal had a large, oval-shaped head which it lifted above the surface and then quickly plunged back underwater. The animal was a formidable swimmer; Papetti was impressed with the speed that the animal reached as it swam. It was as if the water offered no resistance at all.[1]

The size of the animal also impressed Papetti. He claimed, "I am quite sure that this is a strange animal, of not less than 15 meters long."[2] 15 meters is equivalent to just over 49 feet.

Papetti was quick to point out that many other fishermen have observed strange things in the water. Papetti's footage came be viewed at the following web address:

https://www.youtube.com/watch?v=ljzJ2DpWJ1o

Past Sightings

According to Jorge Santi, a policeman, rumors of a strange, large creature have circulated around the community for a number of years. Some witnesses claim to have seen a very large snake swimming with its head above the water. Other eyewitnesses report a reptile that resembles a caiman.[3]

In 1987, another fisherman witnessed a strange creature in the water. Lucio Temporetti saw a giant snake with a big head; it left a large, discernable wake behind as it swam. The wake reminded Temporetti of the wake that a boat creates. After describing his encounter, Temporetti said that had he not been accompanied by others, he would have thought himself crazy. Others saw the same thing—six other fishermen saw the giant snake that Temporetti described.[4]

Though Cabralito received much attention after Sebastian Papetti's video, this was not the first time that the animal was captured on camera. In late November 2011, a still photograph was taken of something resembling the head of a large creature. The local newspaper, *El Tribuno,* published a picture. Many believe the image is nothing more than debris in the water. However, the debris explanation does not sit well with Leo Bonino, who was walking in the area where the photo was taken. Bonino claimed to see the object in the photograph with his own eyes; the object—a large, reptilian creature.[5]

Explaining Cabralito

There are problems when considering the existence of a 49 foot-long, serpentine creature that inhabits the waters of Cabra Corral. As stated earlier, the lake is manmade. Personally, it is hard for me to accept the existence of unknown creatures when the reports come from manmade lakes. Admittedly, though, there are instances where a cryptid may best explain unusual phenomena in manmade lakes. Lake Norman, in North Carolina, and Herrington Lake in Kentucky are a couple of such places that come to mind.

I encourage you, the reader, to examine Sebastian Papetti's video for yourself. In my view, the footage is interesting, but in no way, does it conclusively show a large reptile in the water. The first thought that I had when I saw the creature's head rise and then quickly plunge underwater was that it resembled an otter. Perhaps the wake behind the otter were other submerged otters swimming in a line.

I'll be honest—I hate the explanation that I just gave. The same thing is said by skeptics in nearly every lake monster report that I can recall. However, given the fact that otters do live there, and that the lake is manmade, I believe this explanation best fits. With that being said, though, I do not rule out the possibility that something else is at play here. Maybe even a monster.

Huechulito

Lago Huechulafquen, a glacial lake set against the beautiful landscape of Patagonian Argentina, is home to a lake monster. The lake provides adequate space for a large aquatic cryptid; its surface area covers 40 square miles. Lake Huechulafquen reaches great depths; the depth of the lake exceeds 500 meters (1640 feet) in some spots. Huechulafquen is a Mapuche word meaning "long lake." This native word provides a good description; the lake reaches a length of 18 miles, while its width is only about 3 miles. The physical characteristics of Lake Huechulafquen resemble many of the glacial lakes of Canada and the Northern United States—long, narrow, and deep.

Photos of a Lake Monster

Though rumors of something lurking in the waters had been circulating for quite some time, the creature in Lake Huechulafquen came to prominence in 2009 when a recreational boater took several pictures that are consistent with "typical" lake monster descriptions—multi-humped, dark in color, long, and serpentine in appearance. The photos give the impression that the creature is large and moves by means of vertical undulations.

Jorge Salcedo obtained the photographs from a catamaran which was positioned about 150 meters (492 feet) away from the creature. Salcedo's neighbor sent several photographs to a laboratory in the United States for scientific analysis.[1] According to Ruben Campos, the Mayor of Junín de los Andes, a town about 25 kilometers (15.5 miles) from Lake Huechulafquen, the photographs appear to be authentic.[2]

Biologist Alejandro del Valle spoke to the press on the matter after viewing Salcedo's photographs. She was able to study four photographs which show three distinctive humps. Valle could not say with any certainty what the creature could be. She did, however, say that the image in the photographs *could* be a "huge water snake."[3]

The Aftermath

Taking the matter seriously and determined to find answers, Mayor Campos assembled a team to study the phenomenon in Lake Huechulafquen. Although nothing of substance came out of it, Campos should be commended for taking the situation seriously. Really, though, the mayor should have acted in the manner he did; there had been a long-held belief among many in the community that something strange was lurking in the cold waters of the lake. In fact, as early as 1922, Emilio Frey reported a long-necked, lizard-headed creature that caused the water to boil when it submerged itself.[4] About 20 years prior to Jorge Salcedo's photographs, border patrol officers shot at a giant reptile. The creature got into the water and managed to escape.[5] Given the history, in my view, the mayor acted exactly as he should have when he assembled a team to study the phenomenon.

Lago Paimún

Lake Huechulafquen has a northern arm connected to it by a small strip of water. This northern section is known as Lago Paimún. This lake is much smaller; it only covers about 11 square miles. Like Lake Huechulafquen, Lake Paimún is also rumored to have a strange creature dwelling in its waters.

The creature in Lake Paimún is known as a Trelque, which may be the same type of creature as a Cuero. This creature, however, is said to live in caves rather than the water.[6] Whatever the beast is called, and whatever it may be, it has been blamed for the attack of a woman who was washing by the shore.[7]

El Cuero

Lago Lácar, a glacial lake in Argentine Patagonia, just a stone's throw from the Chilean border, is home to a strange monster dubbed el Cuero—a Spanish word that translates to "leather" or "cowhide." Lake Lácar has an average water depth of about 548 feet and reaches a maximum depth of just over 900 feet. The icy waters cover an area of about 21 square miles.

It seems unusual for a creature to be named the English equivalent of cowhide; but descriptions of this strange beast match that of a cowhide 2-5 feet long, that has been stretched out. The animal also has a barbless, whip-like tail. When hearing this description, the first thing that comes to mind are the large freshwater stingrays native to South America. However, the Cuero has some distinctive features that differentiate it from the common freshwater stingray. Among these, it supposedly has eyes that sit atop reddish stalks, almost like a snail. Some reports indicate that the creature has two eyes; other witnesses claim that the creature has four eyes; there are some who claim that the creature has eyes all over its body. In addition to the strange number of eyes, and stalk-like eyes, el Cuero is said to have an extendable mouth—some describe it as a mosquito-like proboscis. With this, the Cuero sucks the blood out of its prey. To round out the features of this frightful beast is a set of razor sharp claws that encircle its strangely shaped body.

The Cuero is a vicious predator—and humans are fair game. Accounts state that the monster bursts out of the water and overcomes its prey. It then punctures its victim with its mosquito-like proboscis and drains the hapless body of all of its blood. The unusual monster is said to be able to move on land; how well it moves on land, how long it can stay out of the water, and how far it can move on land is unclear.

Sightings and Stories

Documented sightings of the Cuero are difficult to come by. There are enough legends and rumors, though, to believe that something strange might exist in Lago Lácar. One of the most often cited accounts of a Cuero attacking humans occurred when a mother was washing clothes by the lake. Her baby was sleeping nearby, when suddenly, a Cuero burst from the waters and enveloped the child. The helpless baby was pulled into the water—undoubtedly a meal for the brutal monster. This unverified account is strikingly similar to another—only this one comes from Lake DeSmet in Wyoming. I included the following story in my first book:

> The Crow also have a frightening tale in which a monster emerges from the lake and snatches a papoose off the banks. According to the story, a beautiful young mother was cleaning recently killed rabbits in the water. Her sleeping baby was nearby in a papoose-type carrier. Suddenly, the young woman heard something on the shoreline. It was a terrifying creature—coming out of the water and heading straight toward her child! The monster grabbed the infant in its jaws and returned to the water. The helpless woman could do nothing to save her child.

These accounts, while thousands of miles away, are eerily similar in nature. There are others. The following excerpt, also included in my first book, comes from Nevada:

> As the Paiute legend goes, two sisters were washing clothes in the river. One of the sisters had an infant who she left in the shade as she worked. While the sisters were distracted with their work, a serpent emerged and ate the infant...

These are only two accounts; there are countless others to choose from and compare. Stories told by indigenous people of a monster attacking a child on the shore while the mother is busy working seems to be an archetype. Why? If the various accounts, thousands of miles away, are only myths—why are they so similar? Of course, there is a possibility that few consider— the stories could be true.

Conclusion

The terrible Cuero is not limited to Lago Lácar; rumors of similar creatures are common in rivers and lagoons throughout Chile and Argentina. One of these places is Lake Fatalaufquen. Reports from here make the creature sound very similar in nature to a freshwater stingray. Lakes Lolog, Paimún, Ranco, Carrilaufquen, and Rosario, to name a few, are also said to have Cueros lurking in their waters.

Hueke-Hueke'

In other parts of South America, a creature known as Hueke-Hueke' has descriptions that perfectly match the Cuero. The dreaded Hueke-Hueke' is also blamed for attacking people, particularly children, who venture too close to the edge of the water.[1]

Explanations

What are these creatures, Hueke-Hueke' and el Cuero? If they aren't monsters, then how did their legends originate? Famed Argentine author, Jorge Luis Borges (1899–1986), who wrote of mythical creatures, suggested that el Cuero is some sort of fresh water octopus. In the absence of definitive answers, this guess is probably as good as any.

Aside from the snail-like eyes sitting atop stalks, and the aggressive behavior of el Cuero, the freshwater stingray seems to be the most plausible explanation for the Hueke-Hueke' and el Cuero. Though not aggressive, river stingrays are very dangerous and extremely feared.

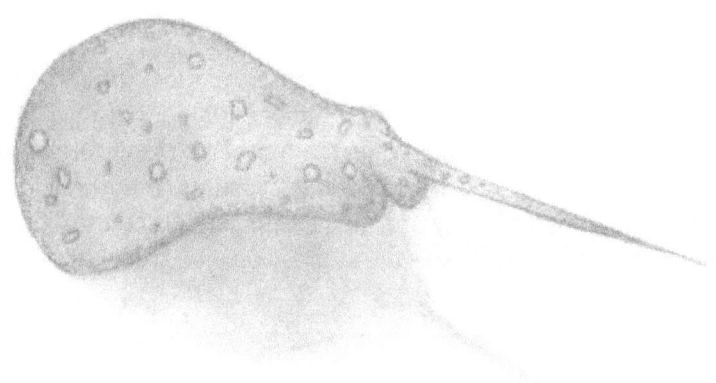

Figure 12: An artist's depiction of a freshwater stingray.

Stingrays are able to inflict a painful, and if left untreated, possibly even fatal sting. The tail of the stingray is equipped with a venomous spine that is capable of puncturing skin and bone. When stepped on or brushed against, the stingray thrusts its tail into its unsuspecting victim and uses the force of its weight to drive the spine. Unfortunately for those who use the rivers of South America, stingrays frequent shallow water and bury themselves in mud and sediment up to their eyes. This, and the murkiness of much of the water that they inhabit make them extremely difficult to detect and avoid. There are accounts of very large stingrays striking a person and the spine becoming lodged in the ankle or leg of the victim. Unable to free their spines, the massive stingrays then swim out into the river, dragging and drowning their victims in the process.

Did the legends of el Cuero and Hueke-Hueke' arise out of a healthy fear for stingrays? This is possible. However, there is one problem with the stingray theory as an explanation for the Cuero. Stingrays do not live in Patagonian lakes and rivers; they dwell in the more tropical and temperate climates of South America. Is it possible that a population of stingrays came to inhabit lakes in the cooler climates to the south? If so, could this have given rise to the Cuero legends? Or is it possible that the fear of stingrays is so ubiquitous throughout South America that the phobia spread to areas where they do not live? If so, could descriptions of the beast over time have been exaggerated to the point of having eyes atop stalks and the other bizarre features of the Cuero?

The Mysterious Lake Titicaca

High on the Andean Plateau, or Altiplano (a Spanish word that means "high plain"), you will find Lake Titicaca, the largest body of navigable fresh water in all of South America. Straddling two countries, Bolivia and Peru, Lake Titicaca is the world's highest navigable body of water. The majestic lake sits at an astounding elevation of nearly 13,000 feet above sea level. The lake is massive; it boasts almost 700 miles of shoreline and its surface area encompasses over 3,200 square miles. At its maximums, the lake reaches a length of 118 miles and a width of 50 miles.

Inca Legends

Similar to the surrounding lands, once a part of the vast and mighty Inca Empire, the lake is shrouded in mystery. Inca creation myths are centered on Lake Titicaca. There are many variations of the same myths; the Inca absorbed many of the legends of the tribes that they incorporated into their empire. What we are left with are jumbled up fragments, probably unrecognizable from the original.

It is said that the Inca believed that the creator god Viracocha emerged from Lake Titicaca in a time of great darkness and civilized the world.

According to legend, after a cataclysmic flood had overcome the earth, the world was covered in darkness. Against this backdrop, Viracocha came forth from Lake Titicaca's waters and created dry land. He also commanded the sun and the moon to rise. After Viracocha's first creative acts—which, in my mind, are eerily similar to the biblical account—he created people. Unlike the Biblical tale of God creating the first man from the dust of the earth, Viracocha created people from large stones. These people were a race of giants who greatly displeased their creator. Viracocha remedied the situation; he wiped the giants from the face of the earth with a mighty flood. Again, the biblical parallels are staggering. The creator god made people once again; this time, though, he used smaller stones and was pleased with his creation—at least for a time.

In other stories, Viracocha is described as a great teacher who taught men all that was necessary to establish a civilized society.

Eventually, Viracocha left; he sailed away, crossing the Pacific Ocean on a raft of serpents.

In other Inca legends, Manco Capac, who was the son of Viracocha and first Inca ruler rose from the waters of Lake Titicaca. Manco Capac, at the command of his father, and accompanied by his wife and sister, Mama Ocllo, went forth with a golden scepter tapping the earth. Viracocha commanded Manco Capac to establish his empire at the spot where the scepter sank into the earth. The scepter sank at Cusco. Interestingly, in the Quechan tongue, Cusco means naval. This is appropriate; the Inca Empire radiated outward from Cusco.

Sunken Ruins

There are ruins in Lake Titicaca that predate the Inca. Archaeologists have discovered an ancient temple complex dating at least 1,000 years old. Presumably, the temple, along with a road, wall, and terraces, were constructed by the industrious Tiwanaku people.[1] These people were indigenous to the area and predated the Inca. In addition to the discovery of the structures, archaeologists have found numerous artifacts in the lake. Ceramic artifacts and others made of silver, gold, and bone have been found.

Rumors of a lost city beneath the waters of Lake Titicaca have been around since the Spanish Conquest. Of course, the Spanish were interested in gold, and it was believed that treasure lay just beneath the cold waters. The renowned French explorer Jacques Cousteau launched several expeditions in the 1960s searching for treasure in Lake Titicaca.

There might have been a lot more going on at Lake Titicaca in prior ages than what were currently know. More perhaps than what we can imagine. Bolivia, particularly the region around Lake Titicaca, is home to large deposits of tin ore. Early Spanish chroniclers noted that there were copper and tin mines that had been worked by the natives in the past. In his book *The Lost Realms,* author Zechariah Sitchin theorized that Lake Titicaca may have been a hub for tin trade during the Bronze Age. Bronze is a metal composed of copper that has been alloyed with about 15 percent tin. Copper is relatively soft; when alloyed with tin, it becomes much harder and more durable—it is more suitable for weaponry.

Ultimately, it is hard to know what took place around the mysterious lake in ages past. Though virtually nothing in the form of records have been left, there is no shortage of legends, myths, rumors, and speculation.

Mysterious Creatures

It is fascinating to think of and reflect upon the hidden history of Lake Titicaca and the mysterious people who inhabited the area in the remote past. But for the purposes of this writing, what concerns us is strange water creatures. In a lake shrouded in mystery, which Lake Titicaca certainly is, it should not be surprising that the lake has its own rumors of water monsters.

It is a common occurrence in the lake and sea monster phenomenon for witnesses to mistake a seal or sea lion for a "sea serpent." In my first book, I theorized that a wayward seal was behind many Igopogo sightings in Lake Simcoe, a large lake about an hour from Toronto. Likewise, as unlikely as it sounds, I believe a Northern Elephant Seal is responsible for most of the White River Monster sightings in Arkansas. How did an elephant seal find itself in a river in Arkansas? The answer to that question is far beyond my pay grade. In the same vein, similar sightings have left some to wonder if perhaps there is a species of freshwater seal unique to Lake Titicaca.[2] Of course, this is pure speculation; evidence to support this theory is lacking.

What isn't lacking, however, are reports of what may be some sort of serpentine lake monster. Some affectionately refer to the creature as "Tittie." There are not a lot of documented sightings to draw from; however, the following report, if true, leaves no doubt that *something* haunts the depths of Lake Titicaca.

A Dinosaur in the Lake?

I found the following account on Chris Parker's website, www.s8int.com. Parker's site is a wealth of information for reports of out-of-place artifacts and living dinosaurs. Parker obtained the report from the now defunct website, livedragons.cjb.net. The live dragons site was run by a Christian missionary who went by the nickname "Dan the Music Man." The following eyewitness report, which occurred in 1989, was told to Dan, directly, by Sue Beecham. Sue Beecham is a pseudonym, as she did not want her identity to be revealed. This is her story:

Stretching our legs on a low hill overlooking the blue expanse of Lake Titicaca, we watched our bus on the small road below, getting its tire changed, when all of a sudden the sound of enormous waves and the displacement of tons of water broke the stillness of the barren country side and stopped the chatting voices of the scattered bus passengers!

Transfixed to our spots, we were frozen with sudden terror, as we watched 300 meters below us beyond the road, an enormous head with dripping open mouth rise from the lake!

It was followed by a 4-5 meter long neck and finally by an enormous hump of a body of a 40-50 meter long... monster!

The 12 meter local passenger bus that we, four young western teenage missionaries, had boarded in Lima Peru to take us to La Paz in neighbouring Bolivia, had been crossing through desolate Andes countryside for hours.

Finally rounding a hill, we rejoiced to suddenly see the blue waters of a breathtaking lake that revealed itself before us; Lake Titicaca, its northern half situated in Peru and southern half in Bolivia, is the highest mountain lake in the world and also one of the deepest!

We finally reached a small town on the shoulder of the legendary Andes lake. Some passengers were released and other local ones taken on. After we left town and had crossed the Bolivian border, our bus had been slowly winding its way along the shoulders of the lake, its choppy waters often lapping just a few meters down the embankment on our left.

We had been watching the deep azure blue colors of the lake waters and the grey mountains in the distance, when suddenly our bus coasted to a standstill! The voice of the driver, announced in the local vernacular, that there was some trouble.

When we had all spilled out onto the road, it was discovered that the bus had a flat tire. The locals standing around, inspired by the view of Titicaca, were soon inspired to swap long yarns with each other about some legendary monster that it is supposed to reside in these waters. Every so often, they recounted, there were renewed stories of people who had sighted the creature, or had heard of others who had.

Getting bored with their tales that soon however turned out uncannily prophetic, we sauntered up the low hill to get a better view of the surrounding countryside. Thank God we did, as standing around gabbing, we were totally unprepared for what happened next! There was a sudden roar, the sound of many cubic tons of water being displaced rapidly, and our eyes riveted themselves on a spot on our right in the lake below, some thirty meters away from the bank along the road.

We froze in our tracks, as we could not believe what we saw.

51

A monstrous head, with a teethed open mouth, dripping with water, half the size of our bus, emerged from the water, followed by an ever growing hump some 20 meters behind its head.

It slowly but forcefully swayed itself from one side to another through the gorging waters, its reptilic eyes scanning the scenery in front of it!

We were gripped with fear, terrorized by the view in front of us, thousands of thoughts shooting through our heads: "This isn't real!" "There are no monsters like that!" "This is ridiculous!" "Pinch me, am I dreaming?" "The dragon of St George?" "A LIVE DINOSAUR?" But they are extinct for billions of years!"

The head rose from the waters on an ever lengthening meters-round neck, forever rising out of the water, as if in slow motion, water running down the grey thick leathery elephant-type skin.

"Oh my God!" We gasped, "We gotta get out of here!" "What in the world, is that?" "Yikes!" "Is it coming for us!" "Oh, Jesus please help us! Protect us Lord!"

The neck swung through the swirling waters, its head 5 meters above the water, glaring at the bus, where the drivers had been working on the wheel, but who were now slowly inching away backwards up the hill, behind the cover of the vehicle, away from the monster, hoping that it hadn't seen them.

The creature opened its mouth and let out a bellowing long wailing cry, faint imitations of which we had only heard in movies like King Kong or other Sci-Fi flicks, only this one was real! It echoed away through the hills.

Its back had now emerged steadily from the water, a rounded mass of muscle power that amazed us by its agility, as it slowly waddled closer to the shore. It moved its 40 to 50 meter long body about, easier than an elephant does his, displacing tons of water in the process!

It had a flattened spatula type tail that got wider at the end which would forcefully flap down on the water, as it dove repeatedly down into the lake.

Our terror gradually subsided somewhat, as we saw that it didn't seem to have the intention to come out of the lake. If it had seen us, it didn't seem to be interested in us, or at least not as lunch for a voracious appetite.

We were never totally sure though, so we stayed on our hill, torn between one desire to see this spectacular sight and another, to distance ourselves as far away as possible from the enormous creature, without drawing its attention too much.

We could never see the end of its legs or members, as the beast never came completely out of the water!—Thank the LORD!

Up to this day I am not sure whether the creature's paws were fins or legs at the end. Finally it kind of went underwater and the bus was started up again and we gingerly boarded while keeping a very careful eye on the swirling waters. And as fast as possible the bus took off and out of there!

Ever since I have learned that there are many watery places in the world beside Loch Ness and Titicaca, where dinosaur-like creatures are still sighted every now and then.

Creationist scientists claim that most of these are plesiosaurs.... But our "dragon" takes the cake, as all these are much smaller than what we saw that day! It was a huge living Dinosaur, 5 times the length of our bus! And at least 20 meters high, as we never saw it fully!

Sad to say, we didn't have a camera on us. But even if we had had one, we probably would have forgotten to take so much as one picture, as mesmerized as we were by this once in a 20th century life-time sight!

If now someone tells me how they believe in evolution and that dinosaurs became extinct 4 billion years ago, I am ever amazed at the thorough brainwashing job the state-sponsored religion of evolution has done on most of the world's population!

Lots of Love,
Sue

PS: If any of the brethren that were with me that day, DID take any pictures, although I don't remember anyone did, please send it in to the following e-mail address:
dan@livedragons.cjb.net

Especially Izzy, also called Elizabeth, sister of Isaac, who lived a long time with her parents in Bolivia! If you Izzy, read this, please contact "Musicman" at the same email address! Or any others who were there!

Certainly, Sue Beecham, and others saw *something* in Lake Titicaca. Something incredible. And why wouldn't this be the case? Lake Titicaca a sacred place to the indigenous people—a place of supernatural origins. More than that, the lake is ground zero for high strangeness in the Andes. Weird lights are often reported around the lake. Strange lights and numerous UFO sightings have led to tales of an underwater alien base. If this is true, the UFOs that people see are also USOs—Unidentified Submerged Objects. With all of the weirdness associated with Lake Titicaca, a resident lake monster seems quite ordinary.

Lake Guatavita

There is a creature, who lives, or once lived, in the bottom of a lake high in the Andes, just outside of Bogotá, Columbia. The body of water is named Laguna de Guatavita, or Lake Guatavita for those of us who speak English. Probably no surprise to anyone familiar with myths, legends, and folklore—or the lake monster phenomenon for that matter—the creature at the bottom of the lake is a serpent. This, however, isn't your run-of-the-mill serpent; this creature is a deity—a goddess.

Lake Guatavita sits high in the Andes at an impressive altitude of more than 9,800 feet above sea level. The lake is circular in shape; it is almost a perfect circle, measuring about a quarter of a mile in diameter. Lake Guatavita reaches a maximum depth of 49 feet; its waters are greenish in color.

It was once widely believed that Lake Guatavita's crater was formed by an impact from a meteorite. Another prevalent thought was that the crater might be volcanic in nature. Today, the prevailing theory is that the crater is really the result of a sinkhole. The sinkhole was created by the dissolution of underground salt deposits; over time, the crater was filled with water and Lake Guatavita was born.

A Serpent, Gold, and El Dorado

Long before the Spanish arrived in the New World with their religious zeal, intolerance, and avarice, the Muisca people were thriving in present-day Columbia. The Muisca were a confederation of Chibcha-speaking tribes. The confederacy was divided into a northern and southern section, each ruled by something similar to a king. In the north, the ruler was referred to as the zaque; in the south, the ruler was called the zipa.

Once a year, the zipa would visit Lake Guatavita and perform an unusual religious ritual. First, he would coat himself in resin. After the resin was applied, he would sprinkle gold dust on himself, completely covering his body. This unusual practice gave rise to the nickname, the Gilded One, from which the legends of El Dorado were born. After covering himself completely in gold, the zipa would float out to the center of Lake Guatavita on a raft made of rushes. What came next really aroused the greed of the Spanish when they heard the tales—the zipa would throw emeralds, gems, and golden trinkets into the lake. Onlookers, probably from the priestly class, cast gold and other precious objects into the lake as well. The zipa then jumped into the lake; his gold dust adornment would wash off and settle on the bottom of the lake providing a sacrifice to the gods.

A commonality among myths and legends that date back for centuries, is that it can be difficult to get a clear picture of the stories, let alone the message that they are meant to convey to future generations. Over time, these legends mingle with other legends leaving us with a hybrid of sorts. Other times, there are two or more versions of the same legend. It is no different at Lake Guatavita; here, there are two variations of the same legend. However, what is clear, is that the events centered on the zipa's peculiar religious ritual gave rise to the legend of the elusive city of gold that the Spanish conquistadors desperately sought after—El Dorado.

Many believe that the zipa was imitating the Muisca god Bochica in the ceremony. Bochica is a diety, some say a sun god, with a long flowing beard. A statue of Bochica stands in Bogotá today. Stories of Bochica, and descriptions of him are similar to the Inca legends of Viracocha and the Aztec legends of Quetzalcoatl. All of these deities were bearded strangers; they were great teachers who came from a land far away in a time of darkness and brought civilization and culture to the people. *

Others believe that the ceremony was meant to appease the serpent that lived in the bottom of the lake. In some accounts, the serpent is actually a goddess. According to this legend, anyone who touched the water would disappear to the lake bottom to be with the serpent goddess. Once a year, the zipa, covered in gold, floated out into the lake on a raft and jumped in, offering himself to the goddess.[1] Perhaps the gold dust covering the zipa served as a sacrifice of sorts as it washed from his body and settled on the lake bed.

What gave rise to the myth of a serpent goddess dwelling in the bottom of Lake Guatavita? What happened in the past that started this bizarre religious ritual in which gold and precious stones were cast into the lake? These questions puzzle me; I wonder too, why are serpent myths so prominent among ancient cultures? Even among two of the most widely practiced religions today—Judaism and Christianity—a serpent myth is prevalent in the creation story; a serpent appeared to

Eve in the Garden of Eden and tempted her to eat of the fruit of the Tree of Knowledge of Good and Evil. The rest, as they say, is history.

Though we can probably never know why the ancients fashioned their religious ceremonies in such peculiar ways, or even how their religions came to exist, we can trace their impact on subsequent cultures. It is believed that the ceremony of the "gilded one" on Lake Guatavita ceased to exist, maybe a hundred years prior to the arrival of the Spanish in the New World. The legend lingered, though, and it piqued the interest of the conquistadors. The legend of the "gilded one" morphed into tales of a lost city of gold—El Dorado. In 1545, the Spaniards were able to partially drain the lake and they found treasures along the edge of the water. However, what they were really after was in the deepest part of the lake; they were unable to reach it. Lake Guatavita has been drained other times, but with little success at recovering the treasure. Today, the Columbian government will not allow any further attempts to drain the lake.[2]

Another Lake Known for its Gold

Lake Puray, near Chinchero, Peru, about a 45-minute drive from Cusco, has its share of strange legends centered around Inca gold. Lake Puray once supplied water to Cusco via a system of aqueducts. According to legend, after the arrival of the Spanish, it became a watery storehouse for sacred golden treasure.

According to the stories, the treasure from the Coricancha in Cusco, and other temples were taken to Lake Puray and thrown into the center of the lake to prevent the Spanish from obtaining the precious, sacred objects. According to estimates, at today's prices, the net worth of the treasure thrown into Lake Puray would be in the billions of dollars. To this day, none of the gold has been recovered from the lake.

Today, UFO reports are commonplace at Lake Puray. A vortex, about 20 feet wide, is said to open and close as some sort of craft enters and exits the lake. Could the legendary Inca gold and the UFO reports be related in some way? Perhaps.

The legends of lost and hidden gold are intriguing. Gold, or tears of the gods, played a fascinating role in pre-Columbian religious beliefs. Why?

* For a greater understanding of the ancient legends of "civilizing heroes" and their similarities across various cultures, I highly recommend reading *Fingerprints of the Gods* and *Magicians of the Gods* by Graham Hancock.

The Monster in Lake Tota

There is another lake sitting high in the Andes in Columbia, Lago de Tota, or Lake Tota, which has a long history of a monster dwelling in its waters. Unlike the serpent in Lake Guatavita, there may be more to this beast than myth—it has been seen many times and sightings date back for centuries. With that being said, recent sightings are practically nonexistent. The creature is deeply rooted in Muisca folklore; the possibility is very real that the monster is not a flesh-and-blood creature, but rather, the stuff of legends.

With a surface area of over 21 square miles, Lake Tota has the distinction of being Columbia's largest lake. The lake is a mere remnant of what was an immense sea in the prehistoric past. Lake Tota reaches a maximum depth of just over 200 feet. Given its depth and its size, the argument could be made that there is plenty of room for a lake monster to call home. Sitting at an elevation of nearly 9,900 feet, the lake's waters are cold; the average water temperature in Lake Tota is about 53 degrees.[1]

Lake Tota's cold water is an optimal habitat for rainbow trout; as such, rainbow trout were introduced into the lake in 1939. Shortly thereafter, Lake Tota became home to a thriving trout fishery. Benefits of the introduction of trout into Lake Tota were far-reaching; not only did local anglers flock to the lake, but tourists were drawn there as well. Moreover, a trout farming industry was born in Columbia, creating much needed jobs.[2]

The Monster in Muisca Mythology

The first known reference to a monster in Lake Tota came from the Spanish conquistador and intrepid explorer Gonzalo Jiménez de Quesada (1509–1579). Quesada had become well acquainted with the beliefs of the indigenous people of the area who spoke of a black monster, said to be a demon, which haunted the waters of Lake Tota. The frightful beast had rendered the waters of the lake impassible. According to local beliefs, Lake Tota was entirely unnavigable.

The black monster, or demon, in Lake Tota is a prominent figure in Muisca mythology. In the native tongue, the monster is called "Muyso Akyqake."[3] The creature was believed to play a role in the origin of Lake Tota. In this creation myth, a monstrous black snake lived in an abyss where present-day Lake Tota is located. The creature terrified the people who lived nearby until Siramena, the great dancer, hurled golden discs at the serpent, which penetrated its scales, effectively killing it. The powerful priest Monetá removed a gemstone from the snake and gave it to the deity Bochica. Bochica cast the gemstone into the abyss, where it landed directly on top of the snake. When the stone made contact with the lifeless serpent, water began to fill the abyss, and Lake Tota was born.[4]

Early Reports of a Monster

A sighting of the monster in Lake Tota is said to have taken place in the year 1652. The Colombian priest and historian Lucas Fernandez de Piedrahita (1624–1688) recorded the sighting in his writings. Piedrahita said that the monster was a black fish larger than a whale, with a head similar to an ox. Piedrahita recorded the following:

> "Quesada says that in his time, trusted persons and the Indians affirmed that it was the devil; and for the year six hundred and fifty-two [1652], when I was at the place, Doña Andrea Vargas, lady of the country, spoke about having seen it."[5]

French explorer Gaspard Théodore Mollien (1796–1872), who spent time in the region, also wrote of the creature:

> "…Superstition has not stopped people these places of grisly wonders: indeed, the wild aspect of the region; suspended waters, so to speak, to such a height and always agitated by the wind blowing Toxillo, higher than the lake of Tota wilderness; mucilaginous substance, oval, and filled with an insipid water in the sand of its beaches, everything tends to arouse surprise. According to the words of the people of the region, the lake is not navigable, the evil geniuses inhabit its depths, in abodes in which, say, porches are when one moves away from the lakeshore was inside, and even You look, they add, occasionally out of its depths a monstrous fish only be seen for a while…
>
> …In the middle of the lake there are some islands; there has been no more than a man who dared to go to them, the belief that the lake is delighted prevents visit…"[6]

The Columbian politician, journalist, and writer, Manuel Ancízar, referred to the monster as "Diabloballen" or "devil whale."[7] Ancízar recorded an account of an Englishman, who, undeterred by stories of the creature, successfully reached an island in the lake on a raft. Upon hearing this, others began exploring Lake Tota's islands by boat and canoe.[8]

Colombian botanist and explorer José Jerónimo Triana (1828– 1890) wrote about residents along Lake Tota who believed in a black monster that inhabited the lake:

> "...a black monster lived in the enchanted waters of the lagoon still persisted among the residents surrounding Lake Tota, in the town of Cuitiva."[9]

Today, sightings of a monster in Lake Tota seem to be virtually non-existent. Moreover, belief in the creature has faded as well. Centuries after the Conquest, many of the indigenous legends, myths, and beliefs have faded into obscurity. However, these myth and legends came from somewhere; what were they trying to say? Could the Muisca legends of a black demon in Lake Tota be rooted in fact? Could there be, or at least have been, some sort of mysterious, flesh-and-blood creature dwelling in the lake? Unfortunately, we will probably never know.

The Nguruvilú

The Nguruvilú is a fearsome, aquatic creature embedded in Mapuche folklore. The Mapuche are the original inhabitants of portions of present-day Argentina and Chile.

The Nguruvilú is alternately called Glyryvilu, Guirivilu, Nirribilo, and many other names. The creature is a "fox-snake," a serpentine animal with a fox-like head and long, spiked tail. The tip of the creature's tail has a hooked nail or claw[1] that is used to inflict damage upon its victims. There is a story of a brave Mapuche man who was able to cut the tail off of a Nguruvilú. The monster's tail measured six feet in length and had a curved nail on the tip.

Legends of the Nguruvilú state that it has magical abilities. Only a shaman can rid the water of the blood-thirsty creature. The Nguruvilú is known for creating whirlpools in the water and causing victims, both people and animals, to fall in; the helpless prey then suffers a watery demise as the Nguruvilú envelopes them.

Reports

Reports of the Nguruvilú are virtually nonexistent today; however, the 1800s and early 1900s saw their share.

In 1806, while trekking across northern Patagonia on his way to Buenos Aires, Luis de la Cruz heard tales of the "fox-snake." According to his guides, the ferocious animal would kill horses.[2]

Jesuit priest and naturalist Juan Ignacio Molina wrote about the Glyryvilu in 1810. He claimed that certain Chilean lakes were thought to harbor the creature, and locals would avoid bathing in those waters out of fear of the man-eater.[3]

In 1915, Chilean folklorist Julio Vicuña Cifuentes mentioned a fierce predator with a slim body and fox-like tail in his writings. The creature dwelled in river pools; when the opportunity arose, it would ambush its prey—both humans and animals—and drag them underwater where it would drink their blood.[4]

The question is, did the Nguruvilú ever exist, or is it simply myth? If it was in fact, a flesh-and-blood creature, what was it? Where did it go?

The Maripill

According to Mapuche legend, a frightening, blood-thirsty creature dwells in volcanic crater lakes in the southern Andes. The creature is called the Maripill.

The Maripill is a large animal that has a saw-like crest running along its spine. The crest is not just for defense; the Maripill uses its crest as a saw to "gut" its prey. The Maripill quickly runs underneath cattle and the crest lacerates the underbelly of the helpless cow. The Maripill has also been blamed for the disappearance of children who have gotten too close to the water.[1]

"Water Tigers"

The South American continent is home to a variety of monsters often described as "water tigers." Reports of these fierce creatures stretch from Ecuador to the Guianas and all the way south to Argentina. Depending upon the region, water tigers go by different names; in each locale, however, the water tiger is a feared predator. The size of the water tiger and other characteristics vary throughout the continent.

Perhaps there is reason to believe in the notion that some sort of saber-toothed cat may exist in the jungles of South America. Ethnologist William Bollaert (1807–1876) found a sculpted rock in the form of a large-toothed cat in Columbia.[1] Saber-toothed cats are featured in the art of prehistoric people from present-day Argentina; depictions of the animals can be found painted on cave walls.

In the 1950s, American author and naturalist Peter Matthiessen (1927–2014) was told of a cat the size of a jaguar that dwells in the jungles of Columbia and Ecuador. He recounted the tale in his book *The Cloud Forest*.[2]

A jaguar with fangs measuring 12 inches in length was killed in Paraguay in 1975. Zoologist Juan Acavar examined the corpse and claimed that it was a Smilodon. Smilodons are saber-toothed cats indigenous to the Americas that lived during the Pleistocene epoch. Smilodons went extinct—allegedly—about 10,000 years ago during the large-scale extinction of megafauna at the close of the last ice age.

A relatively recent sighting of a "water tiger" occurred in the Río Jurumbaino in Ecuador. In 1989, Juan Bautista Rivadeneira saw a creature that was black with short legs and a cow-like tail.

These are but a few tales that fall under the generic "water tiger" category. More specific water tiger types of creatures will be studied in the paragraphs to follow. Worthy of mention, there is a water tiger in Brazil that is called the Aypa. However, documented sightings are tough to come by.

The Maipolina

French Guiana, located on the northern end of the South American continent, bounded by the Atlantic Ocean, Suriname, and Brazil, is home to a creature known as the Maipolina. The animal is said to haunt the Maroni River, where it patiently waits underwater for its prey.

The Maipolina, also known as Popoké and the "water mother," reaches a size of nearly ten feet, has walrus-like tusks, droopy ears, powerful claws, and a white stripe running along its back. The fierce creature lives in caves in the riverbank, and attacks humans and canoes when the opportunity presents itself.[3]

In one of the most often cited reports, the Maipolina was blamed for the grisly death of a child. This occurred in October 1962 when a young boy was drowned and partially eaten after he fell into the water. His body was recovered in the Maroni River near Maripasoula, French Guiana.[4] After the recovery, the boy's body was examined by a doctor. The examination of the corpse revealed injuries that were consistent with an attack by a creature such as the Maipolina.[5]

The Iemisch

The Iemisch is native to Chile and Argentina. It has large teeth, short, dark hair, and a small round head. It is said to be about the size of a puma. Many features make the creature sound similar to a giant otter. Two of those being that it has no discernable ears and webbed feet. Despite the webbed feet, the Iemisch is said to leave feline tracks along riverbanks.

The Iemisch is nocturnal and very aggressive; it is said to attack both people and horses, dragging them into the water. According to at least one report, the creature has a nearly impenetrable hide. Ramón Lista encountered an Iemisch in the Santa Cruz province of Argentina in the 1870s. Lista fired on the animal, but it had no effect; the bullets could not break the creature's skin.[6]

French traveler André Tournouër also shot at an Iemisch. Tournouër lived in Argentina and conducted several expeditions into Patagonia collecting fossils for the Paris Museum. Tournouër referred to the animal as a hymché, and wrote about it in 1900. In a letter, Tournouër claimed that it was hard to separate fact from legend with the hymché because of the superstitious nature of the natives. However, he saw an animal emerge from a stream that matched descriptions of a hymché. Tournouër fired at the creature and it disappeared. Tournouër described the encounter to his native guide, and the guide became frightened. The guide was convinced that Tournouër had a run-in with a hymché. His suspicions were confirmed when feline tracks were found on a riverbank a few miles away.[7]

The Yaquaru

Another animal that falls into the water tiger category is the Yaquaru. The Yaquaru lives in Paraguay and Argentina. It has a dark brown, wooly hide, and a long, tapering tail. The Yaquaru is the size of a donkey and has a long head and large tusks.[8]

Jesuit Thomas Falkner caught a glimpse of the Yaquaru in 1752 while cutting timber along the Río Paraná. He wrote about the creature in his book *A Description of Patagonia, and the Adjoining Part of South America* published in 1774.

"It is described by the Indians to be as big as an ass; of the figure the size of a large, over-grown river-wolf or otter; with sharp talons, and strong tusks; thick and short legs; long, shaggy hair; with a long, tapering tail."

Falkner claimed that when cattle herds crossed the Paraná each year, some were lost to the Yaquaru. Lungs and entrails would later be seen floating on the water.

Falkner went on to say:

"It lives in the greatest depths, especially in the whirlpools made by the concurrence of two streams, and sleeps in the deep caverns that are in the banks."

Another Jesuit spoke of the Yaquaru in the 18th century. In his work *History of the* Abipons, Martin Dobrizhoffer wrote:

"In the deepest waters there usually hides an animal larger than any hunting-dog, called tigre de agua by the Spaniards and yaguaro by the Guaranis. It has a wooly hide, a long and tapering tail, and powerful claws. Horses and mules swimming across these rivers are dragged to the bottom. Soon afterward, one sees the intestines of the animal, disemboweled by the tiger, floating on the surface."

More recent writings of possible water tigers come from author Bruce Chatwin (1940–1989) who traveled Patagonia for six months and collected tales from the locals. He chronicled these in this 1977 book *In Patagonia*.

Explanations

How do we explain the water tigers of South America? What sort of creature(s) could be responsible for the legends? Or, are water tigers nothing more than the product of myth?

Of course, when it comes to cryptids, myth can never be ruled out. American paleontologist George Gaylord Simpson (1902–1984) scoffed at the idea that the iemisch was a real, flesh-and-blood creature, and dismissed the legends outright. He is attributed with saying:

> "Let it be said at once that the Indian tales of the 'Iemisch' or 'hyminche,' if not invented to amuse the stupid white men, were simply myths with no foundation in reality."

Simpson's assertion may be correct; but if so, another question is raised: How did these myths originate? And, what do they represent?

Myths are not the only explanation for the water tigers of South America. One creature that fits the water tiger profile (in some ways) is the giant otter.

Giant Otters

The possibility exists that many water tiger sightings are the misidentification of known species. Of known species, capable of being mistaken for the water tiger, the giant otter tops the list.

Giant Otters inhabit the Amazonian Basin, but their range and numbers have been greatly reduced. In fact, the giant otter is considered endangered; the estimated number of giant otters is thought to be less than 5,000. The Guianas are the only place in South America where giant otter populations remain strong, although the animals are under pressure there too.

It is easy to see how a giant otter could be mistaken for a water tiger. The animals reach about five feet in length and have long tails and large teeth.

Giant otters are carnivorous predators—in fact, they are apex predators—although caimans will prey upon pups. Giant otters often display aggression amongst themselves; however, attacks on humans are rare.

Mylodon

The Mylodon is a giant ground sloth from Patagonia that went extinct around the close of the last ice age. The Mylodon stood at a towering height of ten feet and reached a weight of over 5,000 pounds. The Mylodon had a thick hide—a hide that would have been hard to penetrate; in addition, its skin had osteoderms for added protection. Osteoderms are bony deposits that form scales or plates.

Clearly, if a remnant population of Mylodons survived into the present day, they could be mistaken for any number of monsters— possibly even water tigers. Two things quickly jump out: the size of the creature and its impervious hide. Many water tiger reports state that the creature has an impenetrable hide, with bullets having no effect. The size of the Mylodon, reaching 10 feet, is comparable to the Yaguaru, which is said to be the size of a donkey.

Though it has been suggested that a surviving population of Mylodons could explain the water tiger phenomenon, problems abound when considering this scenario. For starters, the Mylodon was a *ground* sloth. It seems unlikely that a massive ground sloth would hide underwater waiting to ambush its prey. Secondly, and most importantly, there is really no reason to believe that Mylodons survived into the present age—other than water tiger reports.

Smilodon

The Smildon is an extinct saber-toothed cat that inhabited the Americas in the prehistoric past. Like the Mylodon and other megafauna, smilodons went extinct at the close of the last ice age.

Some believe that the Smilodon fits the profile of a water tiger. In many ways, it does. The Smilodon was a large, saber-toothed cat that reached a height of over four feet and was capable of reaching a weight of over 800 pounds. Surely the Smilodon was a fierce, frightening predator! But, did it hide underwater? Aside from water tiger stories, is there anything to suggest that a small population of smilodons is alive today in South America?

Conclusion

Could a remnant population of smilodons or mylodons be responsible for the water tiger legends and stories of South America? As unlikely as it sounds, it makes some sense when comparing reports to descriptions of these prehistoric creatures.

There are other explanations for the water tiger phenomenon. Some believe that jaguars are being mistaken. It doesn't seem, though, that jaguars fully satisfy the physical descriptions and characteristics of water tigers. But then, smilodons and mylodons do not meet all of the criteria either.

If living creatures do not explain water tigers, and if there are not remnant populations of animals thought to be extinct—what are we left with? How do we explain things?

I would offer that perhaps the megafauna that died out at the close of the ice age remained alive—but not physically—instead, they lived on in the legends and oral traditions of the indigenous people of South America. What if memories of these fierce creatures survived in the same way that memories of a global catastrophe have been handed down throughout cultures all over the globe? Like global flood legends and creation myths, water tigers—whatever they were—were spoken of for many generations; as each subsequent recounted the stories, the tales became garbled and unrecognizable from the original.

There is one problem with my theory—*something* ferocious in the water attacks people and livestock...

Camahueto

The indigenous people of the Chiloé Archipelago, an island chain off the coast of southern Chile, have a legend of a greenish cow-like creature with strong claws and teeth, and a single horn protruding from its head. The animal's horn is said to hold immense power; machis (shamans), usually women, use the horn make medicines for treating all sorts of maladies.[1]

Legend holds that a camahueto is born every 25 years. The creatures are born deep inside the earth under a hill by the sea. After birth, the camahueto violently burrows its way to the surface and rushes to the ocean where it will dwell. On its way to the sea, the camahueto scars the landscape with its horn; its magical horn tears into the earth and cuts trenches.[2]

Machis are said to know exactly when a camehueto is being born; they await the camahueto's violent journey to the sea, holding lassos. As the creature makes its way to the water, the machi lassos it and removes its horn. The machi then bandages the wound and sets the animal free. Supposedly, regeneration occurs and the horn of the camahueto grows back.[3]

This unusual beast is most certainly a myth. There are few sightings, at least documented sightings, to draw from. However, legends and myths come from somewhere—how did this myth originate? It could be that the violence of the camahueto's birth and migration to the ocean is a way that prehistoric people explained the region's seismic activity. The story could also serve as a creation myth of sorts—the gouges carved into the landscape by the creature is the origin of streams and other features.

The camahueto as we know it today might borrow from another myth—unicorns. Like the unicorn, the camahueto has mystical powers in its horn. Unicorn legends flourished in Europe; some believe that the Spanish conquistadors brought the legends of unicorns which became intermingled with those of the camahueto.

Water Bulls

A curious phenomenon in South America features reports of lake monsters that are best described as bulls or oxen. In the preceding page, we discussed the Camhuetto—the legendary water bull with a single, magical horn. The Camhuetto, while probably the best-known water bull, is only one of many. Moreover, these other bulls are not confined to the Chileo Archipelago (which is home to *many* strange, native legends), but are found throughout Patagonia and beyond.

In his book *Monsters of Patagonia,* Austin Whittall chronicles a number of water bodies in the Southern Cone that have legends of large mammalian creatures similar to water bulls. In my mind, what makes this phenomenon so interesting is that there were no cattle in South America until they were introduced by the Spanish after the Conquest. Did these animals, strange to the natives, inspire myths that have been handed down? This seems unlikely.

Perhaps, then, water bull legends are some sort of faint, fuzzy memory of a creature that lived in the prehistoric past—these memories, now in the form of myth, are ancient; they predate the end of the last ice age. Perhaps water bulls are not bulls at all, but rather, some sort of large marine animal such as a manatee or even a hippopotamus.

If a hippopotamus, or relative of a hippopotamus, lived (or lives) in the waters of Patagonia, the aggressive nature of water bulls could be easily explained given the notoriously nasty disposition of the hippopotamus. Of course, this is pure speculation...

Various Water Bulls

Lago Cisnes, in the Patagonian region of South America, has been rumored to harbor a strange water creature. Ernesto Bahamondez claimed to see an animal dive into the water whose front quarters resembled that of a cow. Bahamondez described the back half of the creature simply as a water animal. Curiously, he said that the animal walked on the lake. Other reports from Lake Cisnes state that there is a water creature with the front of a cow and rear of a black horse.

The southern Argentina lake, Lago Lolog, has long been rumored to be a place where mysterious beings dwell. Native legends speak of ghosts and dwarves that inhabit the lake. Reports of the Cuero come from Lake Lolog as well; there are stories that blame the Cuero for attacks on children. In the 1960s, reports began to emerge of cow-like creatures in the lake. Sabino Cárdenas spoke of animals that looked like cows in the water that dove underneath when approached. Aldo Peletier is said to have spotted a large, dark aquatic creature in 1984.

Lago Rosario, also in southern Argentina, is thought by some to be haunted by a black bull. According to an indigenous legend, a chief's son was killed by a black bull. In turn, the chief slayed the bull. However, death could not contain the animal—it is heard howling and can still be spotted swimming in Lake Rosario to this day. Interestingly, according to rumor, the lake is also home to a Cuero, and, of all things, mermaids!

Mermaid Legends of South America

Later, we will briefly discuss Christopher Columbus' encounters with mermaids, both in the Caribbean and off the West African coast. Before that, our discussion will start with mermaid legends in South America. The legends of mermaids are more prevalent than you may think; mermaids are said to inhabit both the sea and the continent's inland waterways.

Like the Camahueto, a mythical creature discussed earlier, mermaids certainly seem to be mythical as well. That being said, myths, legends, and folklore get their start from something—they come from somewhere. So, although a half-woman, half-fish creature certainly does not seem to exist—at least not in that form—much in the same way that the magical-horned, sea cow does probably does not exist—these myths still have their place; they should not simply be ignored and scoffed at, but rather, we should examine the stories and ponder the deeper meanings that they are intended to convey.

Circling back to the Camahueto, its home, the islands of the Chiléo Archipelago, are also home to legends of mermaids; the Chiléo islands are rich in folklore and stories of mythological creatures. The mermaid legends speak of a creature called the Sirena chilota—a beautiful, and benevolent creature, said to come to the aid of shipwrecked sailors.

The Yara

Far away from the southern Chilean coast, there are legends of a mermaid, called the Yara, said to inhabit the waters of Columbia and Brazil. Physically, the creature is described as the *typical* mermaid; a beautiful woman with the tail of a fish. The mermaid is said to sing an enchanting song—a song which entices men and draws them to her. The Yara is has been seen sitting on a rock, brushing her long, sometimes greenish hair, waiting for a man to come near. When he does, she lures him in with her song.

According to legend, the Yara has what could be described as a dual-nature. On one hand, she falls in love with men and takes care of them for life.[1] Being immortal, though, these relationships are doomed from the beginning—she is destined to be alone.

Though the Yara seems to be looking for love, on the other hand, she has a very dark side. The Yara is often blamed for missing persons, destroyed boats, and all manner bad luck and unfortunate occurrences.[2]

This legend may be a replacement for an earlier local legend involving mermen. The indigenous people of Amazonia told of a malevolent, male being that preyed upon women, sexually assaulting them.[3] Naturalist Herbert H. Smith (1851–1919) said this about the Yaya (also called the Uauyara):

> "The Uauyara is a great lover of our Indian women; many of them attribute their first child to this deity, who sometimes surprises them when they are bathing, sometimes transforms himself into the figure of a mortal to seduce them, sometimes drags them under the water, where they are forced to submit to him..."

Could it be that the Portuguese and Spanish brought their legends and their folklore with them, which then replaced or at least intermingled with the native tales? The European legends, or at least maritime tales told by those of European descent, describe merfolk as beautiful, seductive females.

Méné Mamma

The Méné Mamma is another therianthropic creature, best described as a mermaid. The name, Méné Mamma, is thought to be a Creole or Quechua word which means "mother of waters." Reports of the creature come from Argentina and the Caribbean, but the best accounts are from the rivers of Guyana.

There are tales of canoes being dragged underwater by strange mermaid-like creatures in Berbice, formerly a Dutch colony located within present-day Guyana. The former governor of the colony, A.I. van Imbyse van Battenberg, spoke candidly of the creatures to British physician Colin Chisholm in 1797. Chisholm recorded the following in his work *Essay on Malignant Fever in the West Indies*:

> "The upper portion resembles the human figure, the head smaller in proportion, sometimes bare, but oftener covered with a copious quantity of long black hair. The shoulders are broad, and the breasts large and well formed. The lower portion resembles the tail-portion of a fish, is of

immense dimension, the tail forked, and not unlike that of the dolphin, as it is usually represented. The colour of the skin is either black or tawny. The animal is held in veneration and dread by the Indians, who imagine that the killing it would be attended with the most calamitous consequences. It is from this circumstance that none of these animals have been shot, and, consequently, not examined but at, a distance. They have been generally observed in a sitting posture in the water, none of the lower extremity being discovered until they are disturbed; when, by plunging, the tail appears, and agitates the water to a considerable distance round. They have been always seen employed in smoothing their hair, or stroking their faces and breasts with their hands, or something resembling hands. In this posture, and thus employed, they have been frequently taken for Indian women bathing."

According to a man referred to as Dr. Pinckard, who is said to have been present during similar conversations in the Dutch settlements, he had heard of plantation owners who were able to corroborate what Battenberg said to Chisholm. Some of the Dutch had even claimed to have eaten flesh from the mermaids. Pinckard also noted that the creatures were held in very high regard by the Indians, who were very superstitious regarding them, and refused to do harm to the strange creatures.[4]

Water Mama

Belief in mermaids persists to the present day in parts of Guyana. Many locals believe in a "body snatching" mermaid that lures men into the water never to be seen again.

In an episode of Animal Planet's *River Monsters,* Jeremey Wade travelled to Guyana to investigate mysterious disappearances blamed on the Water Mama.

After his investigation, Wade concluded that the arapaima, a powerful fish, was responsible for the Water Mama stories. He found that the arapaima there were extremely large and unusually aggressive. The powerful fish has a "torpedo-shaped" body that is capable of inflicting a lethal blow as it lunges out of the water. Wade believed that when the fish surfaces, its long body with a white underbelly—when seen in a brief instant—could imitate the light-skinned mermaid feared by many locals. Moreover, the disappearances were really a classic case of being at the "wrong place at the wrong time." Wade surmised that the victims happened to be hit by an arapaima as it surfaced and their bodies were being finished off by schools of piranhas—effectively leaving no trace of the unfortunate victim.

Wade's theory makes sense on many levels, and it is as good of an explanation as any for the mermaid phenomenon in the rivers of Guyana. Personally, I'm not sure what to think.

Closing Thoughts

I honestly do not know what to make of mermaids and their legends. Listening to people explain mermaid sightings in South America and the Caribbean, it seems as if it is a foregone conclusion that these reports are cases of manatees being misidentified. It is almost stated as fact that mermaids are actually manatees. In the case of the Méné Mamma, this is possible, especially considering that Dutch colonists claimed to have eaten the flesh of the Méné Mamma. Surely, an animal of some sort was killed and eaten rather than a creature that is equal parts human and animal. Still, I cannot get past the fact that manatees, and the therianthropic description of mermaids—a fish-like tail and human face, arms, and torso—*look nothing alike.* That is not to say that I believe in mermaids as they are described, but I wonder: what other explanations could there be? Also, how did these myths get their start?

The Lakooma

Esteban Lucas Bridges (1874-1949), the son of an Anglican missionary, was the third white person born in Ushuaia, often called the "southernmost city in the world," and capital of Argentina's Tierra del Fuego province. Bridges chronicled his family's experiences living in Tierra del Fuego in his book *Uttermost Part of the Earth.* In his book, he also wrote about the indigenous people of the region and their folklore. Among the native people peoples of the Southern Cone were the Yaghans.

The southernmost people of the Americas, the Yaghans, have legends of a strange creature called the Lakooma, who snatches unsuspecting victims that pass by. These creatures dwell in caves, lakes, and bays where they wait for prey. The Lakooma resembles a giant hand that bursts out of the water and grabs its victim, dragging them under where they are devoured.

Bridges recounted an experience that he had in an area known by the natives to harbor a Lakooma. However, he seemed to believe that the legends were rooted in natural phenomenon. On pages 164-165 of his book, he said the following:

> Some six miles east of Harberton is a nest of bluffs about five hundred feet high. They are called the Guanaco Hills, and among them are numerous lakes, five of them of considerable size. During the winter these lakes freeze over, and for two or three months, if the ice is covered with snow, herds of cattle can pass over them without danger of breaking the ice.
>
> In one of these lakes lurked a Lakooma. It was said by the Yahgans that any person venturing near the bank ran the risk of being seized by a gigantic hand, which would be thrust out of the water to grab the unlucky one and drag him into the lake to be devoured.
>
> One winter, when everything was frozen hard, I was crossing that same lake alone, with a load of guanaco meat on my back. Suddenly I realized that I was walking on thin ice, when all should have been thick and solid. Right ahead of me was a large hole. I made a wide detour, and crossed the rest of the lake with the utmost caution. I had been on the brink of the Lakooma's lair.
>
> ...there are strong springs, that coming from a great depth underground, that seem warm in winter and icy cold in summer. It is highly likely that the Lakooma lake contained a comparatively shallow

area, below which was a powerful spring that, by forcing up water of a higher temperature, prevented ice from forming evenly on the surface.

Possibly the local legend arose through some native less fortunate than I being drowned there; or maybe the sight of a hole in that thick surrounding ice gave some fanciful Indian the notion that it was a breathing place for an under-water monster. There are many other places in Yahga-land where Lakooma are said to dwell. One I know of is where a rock and current have caused a whirlpool, which may, at some time, have been responsible for the loss of a canoe with all on board.

Present-day reports of the Lakooma are lacking if they exist at all. Perhaps this should not be surprising given that its lair resides in a remote location at the "end of the world."

A giant hand that grabs victims, is most certainly a myth...It has to be, doesn't it?

Man-eating Fish

South America is home to many stories of killer, man-eating fish. And, why not? Shouldn't a continent believed by many to harbor living dinosaurs and snakes exceeding 100 feet in length also be home to fish large enough to prey on humans?

The stuff of nightmares swims the waters of South America—anacondas, stingrays, and piranhas—and, according to many, catfish which are large enough to snatch unsuspecting victims and drag them to a watery death.

The Amazon River system is said to hold over 5,000 species of freshwater fish; over 1,300 of these are catfish. New species of fish are routinely discovered. Recently, in Columbia, an "armored" catfish, which grows to only an inch long, was discovered.[1] In Brazil's state of Pará, which holds the largest parcel of protected rainforest in the world, a "jaguar" catfish was discovered in 2011.[2] In a protected tract of land so vast, there is a high probability that many more species will be discovered in the future.

The Difficulty of the Water

The waters of the Amazon River system are difficult to study. The waters are muddy; visibility is very poor. Dr. William L. Fink, an ichthyologist with the University of Michigan described the water is in this way: "It is hard to see just a few feet down, and 20 feet down, it's really black." There are spots in the rivers that often have difficult currents making it hard for researchers to successfully use nets to catch fish for research.

Some of the Amazonian waters have features which could easily hide monstrous fish. In the Amazon River, near the mouth of the Río Negro, the river reaches a depth of nearly 300 feet—a virtual abyss.[3] Needless to say, such an abyss presents enormous challenges for researchers.

The vastness of the Amazon Rainforest cannot be overstated. Covering 2.5 million square acres, the immense area, with its thick impenetrable growth, could hold, and hide, nearly *anything*. Though the Amazon is more accessible than ever before, with more and more visitors each year, most people only reach the outer edges of the jungle; much of the Amazon remains remote and inaccessible. Additionally, there are areas of the Amazon that have always been inhospitable—not so much due to the inherent dangers of the jungle, but rather, from the people.

In the early part of the 20th century, Percy Fawcett spoke of the danger that travelers faced from unscrupulous folks in the remote areas of the jungle during the rubber boom. Though it was illegal to own slaves, and had been for some time, slavery was a fact of life on the rubber plantations. Ruthless plantation owners sanctioned slave raids against indigenous tribes. Workers were literally "worked to death;" poor nutrition, the harshness of jungle living, and working far beyond the point of exhaustion took its toll on those who made up the workforce of the rubber industry.

The authorities found the plantations to be virtually inaccessible; hence, the jungles were a lawless frontier less than 100 years ago. In fact, it has been theorized that Fawcett and his son Jack, both of whom vanished without a trace while searching for the lost city of "Z," were murdered at the behest of rubber plantation owners who feared Fawcett would return to Britain and reveal their crimes to the world.[4]

The more things change, the more they stay the same. To this day, much of the more remote parts of the jungle, and the waters therein, remain lawless. Smithsonian research zoologist Dr. Richard Vari explained that researchers and scientists are not always welcome in the jungle. He said, "In Peru and Ecuador, and Columbia in particular, people think this must be some sort of cover for spying on drug traffic. They find it very difficult to believe that you're really out there in these remote areas just to collect small fish."[5]

With all I've mentioned in the preceding paragraphs, perhaps you'll agree when I say *anything could be lurking in the waters of the Amazon River system!*

Colossal Catfish

Several species of catfish in South America are capable of reaching immense sizes. It is hard to know how big these fish can get; locals claim to routinely catch fish that surpass known records. I think that there are always fish out there capable of eclipsing records; there are always "outliers" much larger than we know—these behemoths prowl the waters and should they be caught, represent the next record-breakers.

Three species of large catfish, each highly sought-after sportfish, are the gilded catfish, the red-tailed catfish, and the piraiba. The gilded catfish has a golden color and a distinctive deeply-forked tail. Gilded catfish are known to reach over 100 pounds. The red-tailed catfish, or pirarara, also reaches over 100 pounds. It is easily recognized by its red tail and its over-sized whiskers. The largest species of catfish in South America is the piraiba. These behemoths can reach a length of over 10 feet and a weight of more than 400 pounds.

When Catfish Attack

We like to think of catfish as being non-aggressive; we certainly do not want to believe that they should be feared. For the most part, this is true. However, especially in murky water where visibility is poor, catfish are attracted to movements. When a sufficiently large catfish detects movement such as the legs of a swimmer kicking—this may mimic a distressed or wounded fish—trouble can ensue. Thinking it has found a meal in the form of a weaker fish, the catfish clamps down on a leg or a foot; if the fish is large enough it can pull its victim underwater. Once underwater, panic usually sets in, and the unfortunate victim drowns. This is what I suspect has happened in Oklahoma giving rise to the stories of the "Oklahoma Octopus." This is an excerpt from my first book:

> According to the Army Corps of Engineers office in Tulsa, as of 2008, occurrences of drowning were happening at a rate not seen since 2001. The Oklahoma Lake Patrol reported in mid-2008, that there had already been a 40 percent increase in drowning from 2007. In 2007, a boy who had swam too far from shore started to drown. As the boy struggled to stay afloat, he cried out that something was pulling him down. A rescue was attempted unsuccessfully, and the child's body was never recovered.

Adding strength to my belief, that the Oklahoma Octopus may actually be a catfish, is a report of an attack that occurred over 20 years ago. A confirmed catfish attack occurred in Oklahoma in 1985 in Lake Eufala.

A boy was waterskiing when he tumbled into the water and felt something clamp onto his leg. "It grabbed me and pulled me under the water twice. I couldn't think fast enough to know what to do, I was scared." The boy's mother heard him scream, "Daddy, he's got me! He's got me!" she said. His father dived into the water and rescued his son, and thankfully, the story had a happy ending.[6]

Confirmed catfish attacks have also occurred in Europe. In 2008, a rash of biting incidents had swimmers wary of going into Germany's Schlachtensee Lake.[7]

In 1974, a Hungarian diver was attacked by a monster catfish weighing over 160 pounds. Zenon Grubich saw the large fish swim directly toward him and it swiftly attacked. Reeling from the first blow, Grubich somehow managed to reach for his knife which he used to fend off a secondary assault.[8]

In 2009 another incident occurred in Hungary. A man was helping his friend pull in a large catfish that had been caught when it grabbed his leg and pulled him into the water. Luckily, he managed to free himself from the six-and-a-half-foot giant by kicking it.[9]

The massive European catfish are known as Wels catfish. Steve Feltham, who has studied the Loch Ness Monster phenomenon for more than two decades, believes that a misidentified, large Wels catfish may be behind the legends of the Loch Ness Monster.[10]

Stories from the Amazon

For centuries, natives of the Amazonian region have told tales of man-eating catfish; children are particularly vulnerable and stories of them being pulled underwater are common.

One such incident occurred in 1975 in the Río Negro in Brazil. The story was recounted by Saleceno Valena. Her cousin, who was five, and another boy were in a canoe following local fishermen headed toward a lagoon. Suddenly, a giant catfish struck their canoe and the young boy fell into the water. Though villagers made an attempt to save the boy, he disappeared and was not seen again—not until a week later. A week after the incident, a startling discovery was made—a dead red-tailed catfish was found on the bank of the river. The fish, which was over six-feet long, had the boy inside.[11]

The 26th president of the United States, Theodore Roosevelt (1858–1919) wrote of his experiences in the jungles of Brazil in his book *Through the Brazilian Wilderness*. Roosevelt mentioned the monstrous catfish of the region in his work. Natives in his party had caught a catfish over three and a half feet long. When the fish was cleaned, its stomach contents contained a monkey. According the Roosevelt, he and the other Americans in the group were shocked that a monkey could fall prey to a fish. The locals told him that fish much bigger are found in the lower Madeira; these fish occasionally prey on humans. The following passage can be found on pages 320–321 of his book:

> We Americans were astounded at the idea of a catfish making prey of a monkey; but our Brazilian friends told us that in the lower Madeira and the part of the Amazon near its mouth there is a still more gigantic catfish which in similar fashion occasionally makes prey of man. This is a grayish-white fish over nine feet long, with the usual disproportionately large head and gaping mouth, with a circle of small teeth; for the engulfing mouth itself is the danger, not the teeth. It is called the piraiba—pronounced in four syllables. While stationed at the small city of Itacoatiara, on the Amazon, at the mouth of the Madeira, the doctor had seen one of these monsters which had been killed by the two men it had attacked. They were fishing in a canoe when it rose from the bottom—for it is a ground fish—and raising itself half out of the water lunged over the edge of the canoe at them, with open mouth. They killed it with their *falcóns,* as machetes are called in Brazil. It was taken round the city in triumph in an oxcart; the doctor saw it, and said it was three metres long. He said that swimmers feared it even more than the big cayman, because they could see the latter, whereas the former lay hid at the bottom of the water. Colonel Rondon said that in many villages where he had been on the lower Madeira the people had built stockaded enclosures in the water in which they bathed, not venturing to swim in the open water for fear of the piraiba and the big cayman.

There is a grisly account of a full-grown man being swallowed whole by a piraiba. The incident occurred in the 1990s while three men were fishing in the Amazon. The men were fishing with a net which became snagged on a rock. One of the men dove into the water to free the net—this was a terrible mistake. The man did not return to the surface after he worked the net free from its snag. Hours later, a large piraiba surfaced and was thrashing with a pair of human legs sticking out of its mouth. The legs belonged to the fishermen—he had been swallowed by the monster!

The two other fishermen managed to get the monster onto their boat and they killed it. It measured eight feet in length and weighed 350 pounds. Thinking that no one would believe their story, and possibly fearing that they would be suspected of foul play in their friend's disappearance, the pair took the fish, with the man still inside, to the police station.[12]

Man-eater of the Gran Chaco

The immense Amazonian Rainforest is without a doubt South America's best-known wilderness. Lesser known, and even unknown to a lot of people, is the Gran Chaco, a large, semi-arid, sparsely-populated plain. The Gran Chaco comprises about 250,000 square miles and lies in portions of Brazil, Argentina, Bolivia, and Paraguay.

The Gran Chaco, like the Amazon, is an area where I believe most anything could live and avoid detection by humans. A large portion of the Gran Chaco is covered in swampy land. The water level here fluctuates depending on whether it is the wet or dry season. It is in these swamps that a man-eater is said to dwell.

The Manguruyú

Renowned cryptozoologist, and the "father of cryptozoology," Bernard Heuvelmans (1916–2001) wrote of a slug-like snake that inhabited the Chaco Swamps in Paraguay in his book *On the Track of Unknown Animals* published in 1958. Heuvelmans believed that this creature, said to reach 18 feet in length and over 1,000 pounds, was a giant catfish known as a manguruyú.

The manguruyú is known to pull people under the water where they quickly drown. There are accounts of grown men being swallowed whole by these giants.[13] Indigenous people in Paraguay tell of bathers being attacked, and dogs have been observed being pulled into the water.[14]

Challenges Facing the Gran Chaco

The ecosystem of the Gran Chaco is under increasing pressure from deforestation—mainly for agricultural purposes. Land is being cleared of trees at an alarming rate. Where lush forests once stood, a landscape devoid of trees is now home to cattle which are "factory farmed" for United States based agribusiness companies. Much conservation efforts have been taken in the Amazon, but the Gran Chaco has not been given the same protections. Last year, over one square mile per day of forest was downed and burned in Paraguay alone[15]—obviously, this is not sustainable over the long-term; most assuredly, it will have devastating consequences on wildlife. The manguruyú could become a victim of the effects of reckless land management before it is officially "discovered."

Chapter Two: Mexico & Central America

The Ahuizotl

The Ahuizotl is the legendary water monster of Aztec folklore once thought to live in lakes and rivers around Tenochtitlan, Mexico. Its name means "thorny one of the water" or "spiny aquatic thing." The Ahuizotl is a creature that was firmly established in the legends of the Aztecs. The animal is mentioned in the Florentine Codex, a manuscript compiled in the 16th century describing aspects of life before the arrival of the Spanish.

This strange beast is similar in appearance to a small dog with monkey-like hands. The most unique feature of the animal is a long, slender tail with a human-like hand at the end. Using its unusual tail, the beast would snag its prey—humans—and drag them to a watery demise. The Ahuizotl feasted upon its victims; it was particularly fond of eating the eyeballs, teeth, and fingernails of its human prey. Several days after becoming a fatality of the water beast, the victim's corpse would wash ashore with missing nails, teeth, and eyeballs.

Some have described the Ahuizotl as some sort of guardian of the water. The beast would snatch unsuspecting victims who were in the wrong place at the wrong time—those who ventured too close to the edge of the water. However, this malevolent being went beyond guardianship of the waters; it actually lured victims to the water with cries—cries that mimicked that of a human baby. The creature is also said to have engaged in attacks on boats with helpless fisherman inside.[1]

It was believed that people who died by drowning were taken to the lovely, earthly paradise known as Tlalocan—the home of the water god Tlaloc, his wife, Chalchiuhtlicue, and his helpers, the Tlaloque. Only the priests of the Tlaloque were authorized to touch or remove the body of someone who had been killed by the Ahuizotl. The body was considered sacred to the Aztecs.[2]

What were the legends of the Ahuizotl based on? How did such a fierce animal find its way into the folklore of the Aztecs? Was the creature loosely based on some sort of known animal? The otter is the only animal that comes to mind; otters, however, do not seem capable of producing such legends. Could there have been a creature, now extinct, that gave rise to the stories?

Lake Atitlán

Northern Guatemala's Lago de Atitlán, a majestic lake in the highlands, is revered by the Mayan people who, to this day, live in villages along the lake. It is not hard to understand why Lake Atitlán is considered holy ground; its beauty is second to none. Concerning the splendor of the lake, English writer Aldous Huxley said that it is "too much of a good thing." German naturalist and explorer Alexander von Humboldt declared Lake Atitlán "the most beautiful lake in the world." In addition to the spectacular scenery, the weather is equally amazing. Called the "land of the Eternal Spring," Lake Atitlán experiences a comfortable climate year-round. This is due in part to the high altitude of the lake; it sits at an elevation of over 5,100 feet. The beauty, weather, and the warmth of the Mayan people make Lake Atitlán a very popular destination for expats.

Lake Atitlán was formed by the eruption of a super caldera over 80,000 years ago. Today, the lake is bounded by three volcanos, one of which, Volcán Atitlán, is still active. The lake is the deepest in all of Central America, reaching a maximum depth of over 1100 feet. Lake Atitlán measures roughly 18 x 16 miles, and covers over 50 square miles.

Mysteries of the Lake

There is more to Lago de Atitlán than natural beauty and exquisite weather; the lake holds secrets—at the bottom of the lake, there is a sunken city; more mysterious than that, the lake is said to harbor a nameless dinosaur-like creature.[1]

A Submerged City

There have always been rumblings of a submerged city in the lake; but in 1996, Roberto Samayoa, a recreational diver who grew up nearby, discovered the ruins. There is even more to the ruins than just that of a submerged city; the city actually sits atop a submerged island. Scientists believe that the island was flooded during a natural catastrophe sometime around 250 A.D. Archaeological evidence indicates that the inhabitants left the island quickly.[2]

Researchers believe that the submerged island once held some sort of religious significance to the Maya; several ceremonial monuments and various religious paraphernalia have been discovered.

It is believed the island was a pilgrimage destination that worshipers reached by boat.[3]

The Serpent

The mysteries of Lake Atitlán do not end with the enigmatic submerged island. The lake is said to hold a large, serpentine beast that is responsible for the disappearance of boats and people. According to legend, during the middle of the day, the wind begins to whip around the mountains and volcanos. The disturbance of the wind angers the water; the large serpent of the lake lures boats out toward center and then sucks them in. The creature seems to be prone to aggression; in addition to luring boats and their passengers to their doom, the monster has also attacked people, even when unprovoked.[4]

Many local Mayans believe the legends and are leery of the water. They do not temp fate; instead, they stay close to shore. Word has it that over 300 people have seen the mysterious serpent in Lake Atitlán at one time or another.

It is believed by the locals that the creature resides in a cave. Rumor holds that a network of underground tunnels run throughout the lake and the surrounding area.[5]

If there is a serpentine monster dwelling in the subterranean caverns of Lake Atitlán, then it certainly has a habitat that is conducive to remaining undetected. Furthermore, the lake provides more-than-adequate space and resources. While there are no definitive proofs pointing to the existence of the creature, I would be very reluctant to rule out the possibility of its existence. The lake's habitat is sufficient and there are enough rumors, sightings, and stories to take the matter seriously and be open to the possibility that *something* may be lurking in the depths of Lago de Atitlán.

Lake Nicaragua

Lago de Nicaragua is by far the largest lake in Central America; it is also so immense in size that it is the nineteenth largest lake in the world. The surface area of Lake Nicaragua covers nearly 3,200 square miles. The lake is relatively shallow, however, with a maximum depth reaching only 85 feet.

Over the years, there have been reports of monsters in Lake Nicaragua.

Monsters?

It is hard to say; and, if there are lake monsters in Lake Nicaragua, they certainly do not seem to be the same as the quintessential lake monster so often reported in Canada and the United States—the dark-skinned, multi-humped, serpentine' 30–50 feet in length creature that moves by a means of vertical undulations. However, the lake holds a variety of exotic animals; chief among them are tarpon, sawfish, and sharks—yes, sharks—sharks that have adapted to life in freshwater.

The Sharks of Lake Nicaragua

Lake Nicaragua is a freshwater lake; yet, it is home to a thriving population of sharks. We now know that the sharks that inhabit the lake are bull sharks; for years, though, many believed that the sharks were a unique species—a species referred to as Nicaragua sharks. It was theorized that the sharks became "trapped" in Lago de Nicaragua in the remote past. Given the proximity to the Pacific Ocean, it was believed that sea waters once covered much of Nicaragua. As the waters receded, the sharks were cut off from the ocean by a small strip of land. As such, the sharks adapted to the conditions of the freshwater lake.[1]

Scientists learned in the 1960s that the sharks in Lake Nicaragua are bull sharks from the Caribbean Sea. The sharks access the lake via the San Juan River. Scientists have observed the sharks swimming upstream and jumping rapids[2]—much in the same way that salmon do when they move upstream to spawn.

Bull sharks are one of the most aggressive species of shark. Moreover, they prefer shallow, tropical waters—waters which are often found in densely populated areas. This makes the bull shark extremely dangerous to humans.

Bull sharks have been known to travel surprisingly far distances inland. In the United States, bull sharks have been spotted as far inland as Illinois.[3] That is quite a swim up the Mississippi River from the Gulf of Mexico!

The sharks in Lake Nicaragua have adapted well to life in the freshwater lake. The sharks have thrived and have managed to establish a breeding colony in the lake.

Bull shark behavior is unpredictable. This along with their propensity to swim in shallow waters where they often encounter humans, undoubtedly has given rise to many monster stories. Normally, when a bull shark attacks a human, it has mistaken the person for somethings else. Perhaps the swimming motions of people oftentimes resemble baitfish or larger wounded fish. Undoubtedly, this is of little comfort to victims of bull shark attacks; the swift predators can quickly inflict extraordinary damage to a person.

Though, I suppose, there could be stereotypical "lake monsters" in Lake Nicaragua, it seems more likely that the monsters are something already known to science—bull sharks. However, it could easily be argued, especially by those who have been attacked, that a bull shark is a monster in its own right.

The Wihwin

The Wihwin is a legendary creature, most likely a myth, which haunts the Mosquito Coast of Honduras and Nicargua. The Wihwin is a legend of the Miskito tribe; the Miskito people are indigenous to Honduras and Nicaragua. According Fletcher S. Bassett's book, *Legends and Superstitions of the Sea and of Sailors,* the Miskito Indians believe that the Wihwin is a sea demon shaped like a horse with razor-sharp teeth lining its mouth. The strange creature leaves the water to devour people.[1]

Legend holds that the Wihwin has an insatiable appetite for human flesh. It leaves the sea in the hot summer months and roams the mountains in search of victims.[2] When the rainy season returns, the beast leaves the mountains and goes back to its home in the sea.

The Wihwin shares similarities with mythical creatures from other cultures. The Kelpie, a Scottish water horse, comes to mind. The Kelpie is said to inhabit various lakes and rivers throughout Scotland where it preys on humans. A key difference between the Kelpie and the Wihwin, though, is that the Kelpie is a shapeshifter; the Kelpie is able to take on the form of a human. The Kelpie does not lose its horse-like appearance entirely; it is said to retain its hooves when it presents itself in human form.

Where do these myths come from? Why do people an ocean apart, thousands of miles away, have similar legends of malevolent, horse-like water demons? The question is baffling.

The Panama Monster

In September of 2009, the corpse of a strange creature, similar to the infamous Montauk Monster, made headlines in Panama—and then the world. Called the Panama Monster, the strange creature was reminiscent of the animal that took the cryptozoology world by storm a year earlier.

The Montauk Monster exploded onto the cryptozoology scene in the summer of 2008; photos of the monster went viral. History's *MonsterQuest* devoted an episode to the creature; I even assigned a couple of pages to the animal in my first book. In a very real sense, the world was ready for a strange cryptid, thanks in large part to the creature that washed up on a beach in Montauk, New York.

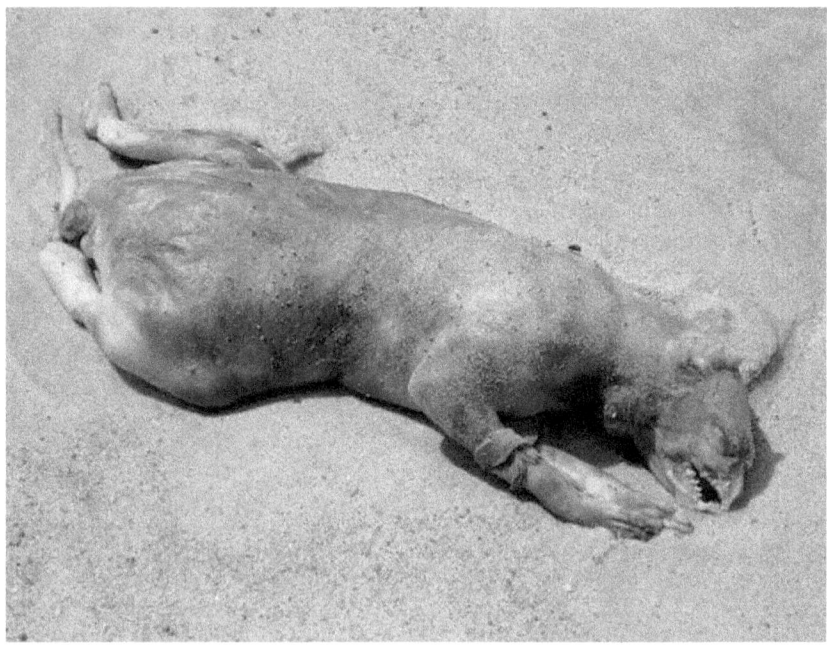

Figure 13: The Montauk Monster.

After pictures of the Panama Creature, or Panama Monster, went public, the creature quickly drew comparisons to the alien being from the Stephen Spielberg film, *E.T.* The weird beast was dubbed "Gollum" in the United Kingdom, after the monster in *Lord of the Rings.* In fact, the animal was described as the monster from the Tolkien book by a teenager who had an encounter with the beast.

The animal was certainly ghastly to look at. It was pale and rubbery-looking, hairless, and had long arms with over-sized, hooked claws.

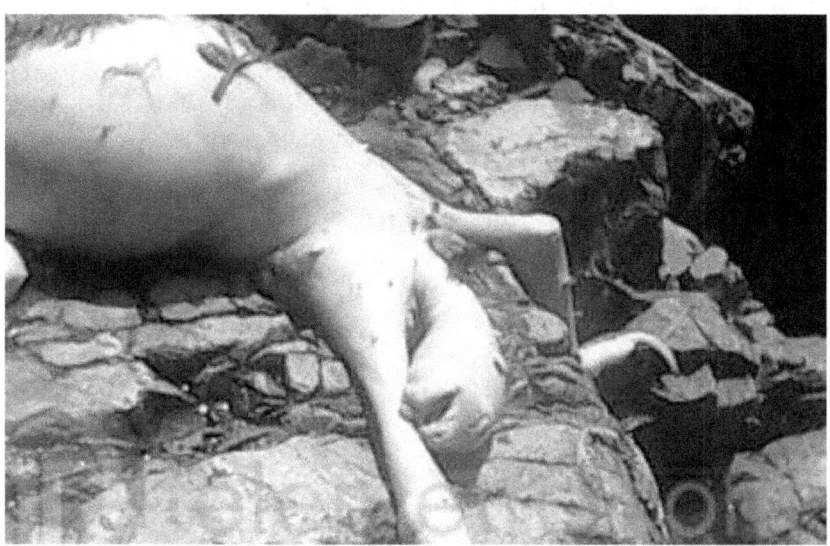

Figure 14: The Panama Creature. Photo by Telemetro.

The creature, whose discovery spread "fear and confusion" throughout the town of Cerro Azul, Panama, was spotted crawling out of a cave by a group of teenagers.[1] The cave was located behind a waterfall on the shore of a lake. The unsightly beast moved toward the teens in what they deemed to be a threatening manner; the kids were frightened for their safety, and attacked the animal with sticks and rocks. The group killed the animal and threw its lifeless body into the lake.[2]

The youths rushed home and told their parents of their encounter with the monster; upon hearing the tale, the adults were incredulous. However, despite their skepticism, the parents returned to the lake with the kids the following day. To their amazement, a strange creature just like the kids described had washed upon the lake shore. The beast was photographed and the pictures were sent to Telemetro, a Panamanian television station.[3] The pictures went viral on the internet.

Speculation on the identity of the creature varied wildly; some claimed it was a genetic mutation similar to the Montauk Monster; others claimed that it was a sloth that had lost its hair; some even put forth the idea that the creature was an alien. Though it sounds outlandish to suggest extraterrestrial origins for the creature, it may not be that big of a stretch for UFO believers. There have long been rumors of undersea UFO/USO bases in the Caribbean.

In the end, the creature was identified as a sloth—at least according to the National Environmental Authority of Panama, who performed tests on the corpse. The smooth rubbery skin was attributed to hair loss from being in the water. It was believed that the sloth had been submerged for approximately two days before being discovered.[4]

Obviously, if the creature lost is hair after its death, this calls into question the story that the teenagers gave of a bizarre animal coming out from a cave toward them. Unsurprisingly, one of the teens offered a different version of events: "I was in the river and I felt something grabbing my legs." He went on to say, "We took it out of the water and started throwing rocks and sticks at it. We had never seen anything like that."[5]

After sorting through the inconsistencies of accounts given by the teenagers, and considering the tests performed on the carcass, it would seem that the Panama Monster was nothing more than a sloth. However, given the Montauk Monster craze from 2008, who can blame monster enthusiasts for getting a little carried away?

Chan

An alleged lake monster from Mexico came to the forefront during the late 1990s when a creature known as Chan began to be reported. The Aztecs were said to revere the creature and the local populace viewed Chan as the manifestation of some sort of "protector god." Every September the locals bring trinkets and other items to the lake where Chan is said to dwell and throw them in as an offering to the god.[1]

Chan dwells in a lake in Valle de Santiago in the Mexican state of Guanajuato. The lake is a water-filled volcanic crater known as La Alberca. According to locals, La Alberca is connected to six other lakes by a series of underground passages.[2] According to some, it is in these tunnels that Chan resides. Interestingly, subterranean passages and waterways are a common theme within the lake monster phenomenon. In my first book, I wrote of many lakes that are supposedly connected to other lakes; in some, cases there are passages leading to the ocean.

Mexican researcher Leopoldo Bolaños had spent much time gathering testimony from eyewitness regarding their sightings and encounters with Chan. Intrigued by the accounts, he decided to travel to La Alberca and investigate the matter in person.[3]

Bolaños assembled a team and they reached La Alberca in September—the very time of year in which locals come to the lake to offer their gifts to the creature. Bolaños and his crew managed to obtain a photograph of the animal; however, the picture is blurry and provides no real proof for the existence of Chan.[4] To complicate matters, other photographs of Chan have emerged that appear in all likelihood to be forgeries. One such picture, supposedly taken from an airplane after an earthquake in 1956, shows what appears to be an Apatosaurus in the middle of a lake.[5] Some have speculated that the picture may be genuine, and that it could be an elephant swimming in the lake. While this *could* be true—a swimming elephant with its trunk above the water *could* explain the photograph—is this a reasonable explanation? Finding an elephant swimming in a Mexican lake would be almost as fantastic as the discovery of an unknown species!

Figure 15: One of the alleged photos of Chan.
http://survivingmexico.com/category/mexican-cultural-stories/

What is Chan? The alleged photographs of the monster certainly aren't very convincing. If anything, they hurt the believer's cause. Something strange may very well inhabit La Alberca, but it probably isn't a sauropod dinosaur.

The Acámbaro Figurines

Though the Acámbaro figurines veer off course from the subject of this book—water monsters—due to their controversial nature and the implications for history if they are authentic, the Acámbaro figurines merit our attention. The Ica Stones were introduced earlier; in the same vein, the Acámbaro figurines clearly depict dinosaurs and, naturally, they are very divisive.

In July 1944, a German merchant named Waldemar Julsrud made an accidental discovery on El Toro Hill, just outside of Acámbaro, Mexico—Julsrud stumbled upon a cache of controversial artifacts. In total, the site yielded well over 30,000 curious antiquities. The relics were from the Pre-classical Chupicuaro culture which thrived in Mexico over 3,000 years ago. Obsidian knives, jade trinkets, and ceramic figurines were recovered.

Significance of the Find

The figurines, if authentic, challenge everything we have been taught about history. In addition to a multitude of dinosaur statuettes, representations of humans—of several different races—were recovered. African, Aslan, Egyptian, and even Sumerian motifs were present. Other strange figurines include a creature similar to Sasquatch, human/animal hybrids, aquatic monsters, and of course, dinosaurs.[1] In total, over 2,600 dinosaur figurines were recovered.

Figure 16: Dinosaur depiction made from clay. Copyright Don Patton, www.bible.ca/tracks. Used with permission.

Obviously, if thousands of clay figurines depicting dinosaurs were fashioned over 3,000 years ago, something is wrong: dinosaurs did not go extinct 65 million years ago as we have been taught; instead, man existed contemporaneously with dinosaurs. Moreover, clay figures fashioned after people of other races, who lived oceans apart on different continents, indicates that there was Pre-Columbian contact in the New World millennia earlier than believed. Simply put, if the Acámbaro figurines are authentic, history is wrong. Science as we understand it is up for reinterpretation as well; the reigning paradigm as it pertains to evolutionary theory cannot be supported if the Acámbaro figurines are genuine.

Controversy Ensues

Conventional thought dictates that there is no way a find such as this can be genuine; the figures have to be forgeries according to the orthodoxy. Unsurprisingly, Mexican archaeologists were quick to dismiss the artifacts as fakes. In 1954, four archaeologists, sent by the government of Mexico, excavated a sight near the Julsrud site. The archaeologists recovered a number of figurines similar to Julsrud's find and concluded that they were authentic. However, when their report was released three weeks later, they declared the collection to be a fraud.[2] According to the orthodoxy, man and dinosaurs did not coexist; it was as simple as that.

Not everyone had such a rigid, unmovable view of ancient history. Professor of history and anthropology Charles Hapgood (1904–1982), who taught at Keene State College in New Hampshire, entered the controversy in 1955. Hapgood is best known for his "Earth Crustal Displacement Theory" popularized in his book *The Earth's Shifting Crust* and his study of ancient maps which depict an ice-free Antarctica; this work is chronicled in his book *Maps of the Ancient Sea Kings*.

Hapgood traveled to Acámbaro in 1955 and conducted his own investigation of the curious artifacts. To falsify claims that Julsrud created fake artifacts, Hapgood excavated underneath a house built 25 years prior to Julsrud's emigration to Mexico. The home belonged to the Chief of Police, Ernesto Narrvete Marines. The excavation yielded 43 artifacts consistent with Julsrud's finds. Radiocarbon dating revealed that the artifacts were not of recent origin; the dating gave an age exceeding 3,000 years.[3]

Hapgood firmly believed in the authenticity of the Acámbaro figurines. In 1973, he published a book on the topic, *Mystery of Acambaro*. There were others who shared Hapgood's belief in the artifacts; famed zoologist Ivan T. Sanderson (1911–1973) believed that the figurines were authentic and wrote about them. Another believer, who accompanied Hapgood on an excavation, was Earle Stanley Gardner (1889–1970). Gardner was a lawyer and an author; he created the *Perry Mason* series of crime novels. Gardner wrote of the Acámbaro figurines in his autobiography. Upon firsthand examination of the artifacts, Gardner declared, "Every criminal, every criminal gang has its own method of operations. Police can often identify a criminal or gang from the method of a crime. It is obvious that no one individual or group could have made the pieces."[4]

Closing Thoughts

Much has been written on the Acámbaro figurines; there is little that I can add. Largely they have been written off as nothing more than a hoax. I wonder, though, have they been dismissed and scoffed at simply because the truth could be too difficult to accept? If they are genuine, then history as we know it must be radically reinterpreted. Personally, I'm not sure if the figurines are genuine or not. But what I am sure of, is that they did not get a fair shake—the fix was in from Day One; the ramifications are too severe—they simply *cannot* be authentic.

Figure 17: Various dinosaur figurines. Copyright Don Patton. www.bible.ca/tracks. Used with permission.

The Yacumama in Mexico and Central America?

Mexico simply doesn't have anything close to the number of sea serpent/lake monster sightings as its neighbors to the north, the United States and Canada. I believe, at least in the case of lake monsters, this is because Mexico lacks the glacial lakes left behind from the last ice age that dot the landscape of the northern United States and Canada.

With that being said, Mexico has had its share of sightings of sea serpents and lake monsters which warrant attention; however, sightings are sporadic—so sporadic in fact, that some of the creatures have not even earned nicknames. I believe that the possibility exists that various sea serpent reports from Mexico may be explained by a creature that was covered in the South America chapter—the Yacumama.

Noteworthy Reports

A lake monster report from Lago Catemaco was recorded in 1969. According to witnesses, a large, serpentine creature, black in color, was observed. **The creature had two horns**.[1]

In June 1908, north of Frontera, in the waters of the Gulf of Mexico, a sea serpent was spotted by the crew of the *Livingston*. Witnesses claimed the creature was **200 feet long and 3 feet in diameter**. As it swam away, it made a sound similar to a Gatling gun.[2]

Thinking out Loud

Thinking of the 1908 sighting north of Frontera and the 1969 report from Lago Catemaco, a question came to mind: could a Yacumama be responsible for the sightings? Could the creature, native to central South America, make such an unlikely journey?

When researching the Minhocão, which I believe is the same creature as the Yacumama, I learned that in Nicaragua there are reports of a large, burrowing, snake-like creature that resembles the Minhocão. If the reports are true, the range of the Yacumama extends much further north than what I had initially believed.

It may sound outlandish to suggest, but the size of the creatures match, or even exceed, that of a Yacumama. Moreover, in email correspondence with Mike Warner, he told me that Yacumamas can live in both salt and freshwater.

Admittedly, my observation stretches the bounds of believability to the breaking point—there really is no reason to believe that a Yacumama was spotted at sea. Still, the size of the sea serpent jumped out at me, and a Yacumama could conceivably reach that size. Although Yacumamas can live in saltwater, I'm not sure it is reasonable to think that one could be spotted fifty miles offshore as was the case in the 1908 sighting.

The Lake Catemaco sighting matches the Yacumama quite well. Note that the creature was large, dark-colored, and had horns.

Of course, the sightings could be explained in any number of other ways—each probably being more reasonable than what I suggested. However, the more I thought about it, I wondered—could sightings of sea serpents in Mexico be the basis for ancient legends?

The Plumed Serpent

Lake Catemaco, in Veracruz State, is about a five-hour drive from Frontera, in Tabasco State. Both are located at ground zero for high, advanced civilization in ancient Mesoamerica.

Though legends vary, both the Aztecs and the Maya told of a deity that took the form of a plumed serpent. To the Aztecs, this god was known as Quetzalcóatl. To the Maya, the serpent god was known as Kukulcán. To the K'iché Maya, who inhabit the highlands of Guatemala, the feathered serpent is named Q'uq'umatz.

Figure 18: Feathered serpent statue in the National Museum of Anthropology in Mexico City. By Thelmadatter - Own work, Public Domain, https://commons.wikimedia.org/w/index.php?curid=3744871

In some of the legends, Quetzalcóatl is a man—a bearded high priest who forbade the sacrifice of humans, but instead, offered sacrifices of birds, flowers, and butterflies. In an epic struggle of good versus evil, good was defeated and Quetzalcóatl was banished from the land by the evil god Tezcatlipoca, also known as "smoking mirror." Quetzalcóatl made his way to the coast and sailed away on a raft of serpents; before he left, he promised his followers that he would return someday.

It is believed that because of the legends of the benevolent, bearded Quetzalcóatl, and his promised return, the Aztecs may have been caught off guard when Hernán Cortés and his band of conquistadors landed on the Yucatán Peninsula in the early 1500s. The Spanish quickly dismantled the civilization of the Aztecs—they burned their writings; destroyed their temples; took their gold; and forbade the practice of their religion.

Figure 19: Serpent depiction at the Temple of the Feathered Serpent in Teotihuacan. Photo by Jami Dwyer. http://www.flickr.com/photos/jamidwyer/2844706070/in/set-72157606952714490/

A Factual Basis?

Could the legends of a plumed serpent have some sort of vague, distant connection to something real? Could the likenesses of the deities Quetzalcóatl, Kukulcán, and Q'up'umatz be based on something that had been observed by the ancestors of the Aztecs and the Maya? More specifically, could the mighty Yacumama, the colossal snake, have served as a model for the legends?

If the Yacumama exists, and I believe that it does, there is no reason to believe that that does not, or at least did not, live in the jungles of Mexico. Mike Warner has suggested that these gargantuan snakes were once more widespread than they are today, and that their range reached far beyond South America.

The "Sierpe"

As mentioned earlier, legends in Nicaragua tell of a burrowing monster that is very large and snake-like. The following article, from 1878, is titled "Underground Monsters," and was printed in the science journal, *Nature:*

> In a former number (vol. xvii. p. 325) we gave some account of a curious underground monster, the Minhocao, supposed to exist in. Brazil. Dr. Spencer Baird, of the Smithsonian Institution, sends us an interesting document, which shows that the belief in such a monster is not confined to Brazil, but is shared in by the people of Nicaragua. In the Gaceta de Nicaragua for March 10, 1866, is a long letter signed "Paulino Montenegro," containing a circumstantial account of an object possessing very much the same attributes as the Minhocao. The letter is dated Jinotega, Nicaragua, February 21, 1866. The writer states that he went to Concordia on private business, when he heard on the 17th of a serpent having taken up its abode at a place called La Cuchilla, within the jurisdiction of the village. Along with some friends, M. Montenegro set out on the 18th to examine into the foundation of the report. A tradition concerning such a monster has existed from "time immemorial." After having travelled on that day about two leagues (1 league = 2-6 English miles) north-east from the village, they reached the spot where the inhabitants of the neighbour hood had traced signs and tracks, which, M. Montenegro states, positively prove the existence of such an animal.
>
> The most detailed accounts stated that here, some five years before, a sort of platform of about fifty varas diameter had been formed at the foot of a large rock cropping out from a hillside. One of the neighbours had established there an orchard, though no one had been able to account for this new formation. Three years before, however, people began to observe that this little piece of level ground was gradually deepening, and that in the month of November the base of the rock adjoining it became exposed and worn from some agency, notwithstanding that there was not sufficient water to cause the phenomenon. At the same time mighty trees (roblts) were observed to become uprooted and to fall in great disorder, while immense rocks were moved and shifted their foundations so much, that in the following month of December, during one night, the road from Chichiguas and Cuchilla to San Rafael del Norte was destroyed by a multitude of cracks and clefts, which had suddenly opened. At that time the ground was observed to be undermined, falling in at intervals. These occurrences were observed some three days before M. Montenegro and his friends visited the place, which they saw all to be in accordance with the

statements. Immediately on examining the locality for themselves they came to the conclusion that there were signs not of one but of two animals, probably of the shape of huge fishes.

In commencing their work these animals seemed to pursue a kind of an upheaving movement. As the bottom of their hiding-place was loose, shifting ground, the surface of this was seen to give way, while trees were shaken out and came down crashing. The noise of this seemed to scare the animals away. One of them — believed to have been the male on account of its larger size and greater strength — took to the left in descending, but always in a parallel direction with and along the slope of another hill, which here terminated. As it broke through the banks of a ravine, which measured about twenty varas in width and nine feet in depth at its greatest opening, he passed with his head underground. The thrown-up soil showed the tracks of the head, which left its marks both in the soil and on the roots of the trees, which were broken, the broken pieces being four inches thick. The main part of the body, which certainly must have passed here uncovered, left its traces at the bottom of the ravine. Passing out from this the animal entered upon ground more level and friable, which it went through at a depth of five quarters (1.25 varas), forming a furrow and leaving behind a ridge more than one vara high. Following the ravine for a distance of about sixty varas it encountered two deep ditches, when it turned and traced its way back, and, approaching the aforesaid ravine, took to the bed of a pond and disappeared perpendicularly.

The other animal, which left behind a smaller track, and therefore was believed to have been the female, went at once to the right, to the outlet of the pond of water before referred to, leaving behind it everywhere the same marks as the other. When it reached the two deep ditches it turned back also, and undoubtedly encountered its companion afterwards.

The whole ground had become irregularly disturbed and broken up, and the power of these animals is shown by their being able not only to throw up huge masses of soil but even to move rocks weighing more than thirty quintals.

The animals seem to be covered with a skin clad with scales or plates, the markings of which, imprinted on the soft clay or loam, bear much resemblance to those of the garrobo I in the mud. It appears that the shape of these animals must be like that of the guapote. The length of the body is at least twelve varas, the height three, and its thickness 1.5 varas.

A tradition about such an animal as this has been kept up unaltered, without contradiction, for more than a hundred years. It is described in general as a large snake, and called "sierpe," on account of its extra ordinary size, and living in chaquites. One is said to have been once killed by lightning the moment it had left its hiding-place in the river "Sebaco viejo."

Comparisons are drawn between the Nicaraguan creature and the Minhocão in another article from the 1800s. The following is from the science journal *Knowledge,* printed on May 26, 1882:

The attention of the public is from time to time called to the supposed existence of a sea-serpent of enormous size, and the question of its existence has of late found a place in your columns. Probably few people have heard of the Minhocao, a worm of, according to some accounts, fifty yards length, and five yards breadth, covered with bones as with a coat of armour, and in its burrowings rooting up mighty trees, diverting courses of streams into fresh channels, throwing up heaps of earth, and in its course making trenches about three metres in breadth. The reports of this animal, which has its existence in the highlands of the southern provinces of Brazil) seem well authenticated, and are as marvellous as those of the sea-serpent, if not more so. The accounts, however, as to the size and appearance of the animal are uncertain. It is supposed to be a relic of the race of gigantic armadilloes, which in past geological epochs are said to have been abundant in South Brazil.

The belief in this monster is not confined to Brazil, but is shared in by the people of Nicaragua, where a tradition of such a monster has existed from time immemorial; and as recently as the year 1866 a Nicaraguan Gazette gives a circumstantial account of an object much the same as the Minhocao. The accounts, however, of the Minhocao of Brazil are still more recent.

I have read that the Romans in their wars with the Carthaginians are said to have fallen in with a serpent 120 feet long, which dwelt upon the banks of a river and had tough scales.

As the existence of such an animal seems as interesting a subject of inquiry as that of the sea serpent, perhaps Knowledge may admit inquiries on the subject.

With reports of massive snakes in Nicaragua, and sightings in Mexico, it seems plausible that the ancient legends of a plumed serpent deity are based on something very real—the Yacumama, the nightmarish, colossal snake that also haunts the jungles of South America.

Chapter Three: The Caribbean

Lusca

The Caribbean is home to a colossal beast, thought to be a gigantic octopus-like creature, called the Lusca. Some claim that the Lusca is half octopus, and half shark; others state that the beast is half squid and half eel. Some have said that the Lusca is a terrible, multi-headed creature. The Lusca is a truly terrifying creature; the animal is said to measure 75 feet in length, and lengths of 200 feet have been reported. By contrast, the largest known giant Pacific octopus *only* reached a length of about 30 feet.

Like an octopus, the Lusca is said to be able to change its color— natural camouflage gives the mighty Lusca, already an apex predator, a huge advantage.

Is the Lusca rooted in legends of the "mythical" kraken, or is the reverse true? Are they one in the same? Myths and legends get their start somewhere; could there actually be an enormous species of octopus stalking the great deep?

Sightings and Habitat

Actual sightings of the Lusca are rare. According to reports and folklore, the gargantuan octopus hunts at night, especially when the moon is full; this is when it surfaces and snatches its prey. The creature has been known to not only prey on marine animals, but unfortunate divers and boaters have fallen victim to the beast.

The mystifying giant is said to inhabit areas of the Caribbean that are known as blue holes. Blue holes are giant steep-walled sinkholes in the ocean that have formed limestone reefs along the top. Typically, blue holes have openings that are circular in shape. The holes are extremely deep, and in many cases, they provide access to a system of underwater caverns and passages.[1]

The animal is also thought to dwell in the "tongue of the ocean," a trench about 20 miles wide by 150 miles long that reaches depths of over 6,000 feet.

It is out of these seemingly bottomless oceanic pits—the blue holes, and the abyss known as the tongue of the ocean, that the Lusca comes to the surface to claim its victims. It has been said that the Lusca has used its exceedingly long tentacles to snatch unsuspecting victims off of the beach dragging them into the blue holes never to be seen again.[2]

Witnesses have claimed to see bubbles and swirling water as the Lusca sucks boats and victims down to their doom. Later, it "regurgitates" the wreckage. Scientists familiar with blue holes attribute the "sucking and regurgitating" of the Lusca to natural phenomenon—tidal movements—rather than an enormous killer octopus.

Globsters

Large, unidentifiable, organic masses that mysteriously wash up onto beaches—nicknamed globsters—are often attributed to the Lusca. Globsters are often thought to be the remains of giant octopuses and giant squids. Sometimes, globsters turn out to be beaked whales and basking sharks; it is not unusual though, when the remains simply cannot be identified.

One of the most famous globsters washed up onto a Florida beach in 1896. Dubbed the St. Augustine Monster, this globster, originally thought to be the remains of a giant octopus, is one of the earliest documented "blobs".

Figure 20: The St. Augustine Monster.

In 1971, Dr. Joseph F. Gennaro Jr. performed tissue analysis on the St. Augustine monster and concluded that the specimens were consistent with that of an octopus. Famed cryptozoologist Roy P. Mackal conducted testing of his own in 1986; his results confirmed the work of Dr. Gennaro.[3]

Later analysis of samples from the St. Augustine Monster creature called into question the findings of Mackal and Gennaro. The most recent results indicate that the specimens are consistent with whale blubber.

Do globsters, the nondescript blobs which mysteriously wash upon beaches, provide evidence for the Lusca? Perhaps. But at this point, the hard evidence is lacking. However, when taken together with centuries of folklore and legends, the case becomes much stronger. Making the case even stronger is the fact that so much of the ocean remains unexplored. We have better maps of the surface of Mars than the ocean floors on our own planet.

What could be lurking deep within the blue holes and oceanic trenches? We simply cannot say. Who is to say a gargantuan octopus could not exist?

The Creature from San Miguel Lagoon

In 1971, an unusual creature was spotted in a lagoon outside of Havana, Cuba. The lagoon, a flooded quarry, is located in San Miguel del Padrón, a suburb of Havana. Rumors of a frightening creature quickly spread throughout Havana; crowds of curious onlookers flocked to the lagoon. As news of the monster spread, the masses grew—crowds that once were in the hundreds, quickly escalated to thousands in number. The creature created such a buzz within the community, that the government-ran radio station, Radio Progresso, took an interest and sent reporters to investigate. The correspondents descended upon the scene; they examined eyewitness reports and interviewed witnesses.

Descriptions of the creature vary; some described it as spindle-shaped, with large and threatening yellow eyes; others claimed to see a horned, hippopotamus-like animal with a featureless face. According to one witness who claimed to have seen the animal on multiple occasions: "It doesn't look like anything but a black ball that, maybe, resembles a hippopotamus with horns, but it doesn't really resemble any animal...and it's got no eyes on it at all."[1]

One of the reporters sent to investigate the phenomenon saw the creature for himself. He claimed to see something rise from the water amid "intense bubbling." Whatever this animal was, it had a rough texture and a rounded shape. After it surfaced, it floated for a few seconds, and then sank back into the water.[2]

Psychic Abilities?

If some of the stories about the monster are true, then we have a very strange creature—one that may have psychic abilities. Rumors tell of an elderly man who lived in a ramshackle home by the lagoon that was driven crazy by the monster. According to the story, after the man encountered the creature, he fled in terror. The poor man had gone mad instantaneously and later hanged himself from a tree.[3]

Word spread of the monster's mind-bending abilities. Many of the folks who ventured to the lagoon shielded their eyes, careful not to make eye contact with the creature—fearful of its dreaded gaze.

Explanations

What are we to make of the creature from San Miguel Lagoon? The tales are fantastic; surely *something* could have been in the lagoon, but did that *something* have psychic abilities? Probably not. This aspect of the tale is probably nothing more than an embellishment—much like a fish story. What probably started out as someone seeing something that they couldn't explain, quickly morphed into a larger-than-life tale.

An explanation for the identity of the creature has been offered—an explanation that is all too common—misidentification. In this case, the misidentification of inanimate objects is blamed. The objects: tree trunks.

A man who worked at the lagoon making charcoal was very skeptical of the stories. He said, "I've never seen anything in the 10 or 11 years I've been here." The collier offered an explanation for hysteria: people were seeing palm trunks. He said, "Three or four months ago, some trucks, a fleet of trucks came here and dumped palm trunks in the water."[4]

The question becomes, is the collier's story a reasonable explanation for the phenomenon? Maybe. But it is tough for me to believe that hundreds, even thousands of people were mistaking tree trunks for an animal. But, I suppose it is possible; stranger things have happened...

Huilla

A monster of sorts is known to frequent the waters of Trinidad & Tobago, particularly Trinidad's Ortoire River. The Ortoire is the largest river in the twin island nation, and is known for its occasional bioluminescent glow which turns the water a brilliant shade of blue. What concerns us, though, is the monster; a massive serpent, large enough to prey on alligators. According to reports, not only is the creature able to attack alligators, it has been observed attacking both alligators and caimans.

The creature in question is described as green in color, scaly, serpentine in appearance, with a horse-like head. The animal is massive; it is said to reach a length of up to 50 feet![1] Aside from the animal's immense size, its description matches that of a known animal, one that is native to the region—the green anaconda. In fact, huilla (pronounced 'weel') is one of the local names for the green anaconda. It is also called a water boa.

Eunectes murinus

The green anaconda, *Eunectes murinus,* a member of the boa family, is the largest species of anaconda. Capable of reaching lengths of 30 feet, and a body diameter of over a foot, the colossal serpents can reach weights exceeding 550 pounds.

There is another type of snake that could not only reach, but surpass the 50 feet length that has been reported in Trinidad—this is the "giant anaconda." The giant anaconda, which I believe is the Yacumama—covered at length earlier in this book—is an apex predator which could easily dwarf the green anaconda.

The 1997 film *Anaconda* comes to mind. The movie, starring Ice Cube and Jennifer Lopez, chronicles a pair of a film crew members shooting a documentary in the Amazon. As the story unfolds, they end up being terrorized by a giant Anaconda.

Sightings, Stories, and More

Stories of the massive Huilla did not stay in Trinidad & Tobago for long. Tales of the gargantuan serpents reached Britain in the days when Trinidad & Tobago was a colony of the Crown. The *Straits Times* said this in 1934:

...a scaly serpent estimated to be 30 feet long was authentically reported to have been seen rising in three arches in the East Coast River, Trinidad.

The existence of such a monster is officially recorded in the annals of the Colony, for there exist photographs showing a monster 25 feet long which is known locally as huilla, and which swallowed an alligator.

Is the monster-sized snake, known locally as a huilla, spoken of in the newspaper report a green anaconda? It fits the profile and matches descriptions well. With that being said, though, there are huilla reports in which witnesses describe characteristics that are not common to the green anaconda.

One characteristic of the monster in question is that it leaves three-toed tracks along the banks.[2] The monster also is said to migrate between water bodies; presumably, it has the ability to walk across land. Although anacondas move across land between different waterways, they are somewhat ungainly and are only able to move at about half the speed that they are able to reach in the water. It goes without saying that anacondas do not leave three-toed tracks.

There is another peculiar trait that has been associated with the monster—it emits a high-pitched whistle.[3] Obviously, snakes are not known for making whistling sounds. However, this is not without precedent when dealing with cryptids, especially sea serpents. In my first book, I included the following report from the Great Lakes:

In 1892, a Chicago based newspaper reported that a group of women were frightened by a large, snake-like creature while bathing in the water. According to the women, the snake was black and had an oily appearance. Although the snake never threatened the ladies—it didn't seem to notice them—they still fled in fear. The creature is said to have made a "whirring" noise as it passed.

It is not clear, at least to me, if the huillas of Trinidad & Tobago are simply green anacondas—monsters in the own right—or if the name huilla encompasses the anaconda *and some sort of water monster*. If it is true that a creature makes whistling sounds and leaves tracks, then it surely is something other than a snake, even a snake of gargantuan proportions. If these reports are not true, and if what people are seeing doesn't reach lengths of 50 feet, then where do these stories come from? Are the reports nothing more than embellishments of an already frightening creature? Maybe. But still, it might be worth keeping an open mind to the idea that something strange might be haunting the waters of Trinidad & Tobago.

The Caribbean Monk Seal

I feel compelled to write, even if it is only briefly, about the Caribbean monk seal and its place among cryptid reports in "South of the Border." I believe that this species of seal, now officially extinct (though sightings still occur), may be responsible for at least a few sea serpent sightings from time to time.

The Caribbean monk seal, also known as the West Indian monk seal, once flourished in the Caribbean with at least 13 breeding colonies. Of course, the seals were a favorite food of the sharks living in the water; but it was another predator that ultimately brought about the demise of the Caribbean monk seal—humans.

Shortly after Christopher Columbus arrived in the New World, it did not take long for Europeans to begin overhunting the seals. As more settlers came to the area, oil from seal blubber became a valuable commodity. The oil was used for lamps and for cooking. The problem was greatly exacerbated as sugar plantations became operational. Much of the machinery used seal oil as grease and lubrication for moving components.

The easily approachable, docile creatures were easy prey; often, as nursing mothers lay on the beach tending to their pups, sailors and hunters would walk up and club them to death. It has been said that as many as 100 seals would be harvested in a single night. The Caribbean monk seals were not able to recover once their population had been decimated. In 1952, between Jamaica and Nicaragua, the last confirmed Caribbean monk seal sighting occurred. In 1967, the seals were placed on the list of endangered species; they were officially declared extinct 41 years later—tragically, their extinction was a direct result of human activity.

Why am I burdening you, the reader, with this tragic tale? Don't you get enough with the heart-rending Society for the Prevention of Animal Cruelty commercials? If not, seeing regular pictures from CNN of emaciated polar bears clinging to small blocks of ice surely tugs at the heart strings. Why bring it up? Simple—it is impossible to tell the tale of the Caribbean monk seal without discussing their tragic demise. With that being said, though, I believe that there may be a surviving remnant—albeit a very small one.

Seals Masquerading as Sea Serpents

Seals have a long, storied history of being the impetus behind sea serpent and lake monster phenomena. In *People are Seeing Something: A Survey of Lake Monsters in the United States and Canada,* I advanced the theory that reports from the 1930s and 1970s of Arkansas' White River Monster can be attributed to a wayward northern elephant seal. As preposterous as this sounds, it was the only conclusion I could reach. Likewise, when studying the reports of a creature from Ontario's Lake Simcoe, dubbed the Igopogo, I also concluded that a seal was responsible. It is my belief that an incredibly lost seal made an unlikely journey from the ocean to the St. Lawrence River, moving from lake to lake until being spotted in Lake Simcoe—and subsequently being misidentified as a monster. These, of course, are extreme—no, *very* ex*treme, vastly improbable examples.

Could there be marine mammals, perhaps related to seals, which are presently unknown to science? This is what the Dutch zoologist, A.C. Oudemans (1858–1943) concluded in his legendary work, *The Great Sea-Serpent.* Oudemans believed that a large marine mammal, a previously unknown seal, was responsible for sea serpent sightings and legends. The creature was dubbed *Megophias megaphias.* Although Oudemans' speculative large marine mammal has yet to be proven, the thought is intriguing nonetheless.

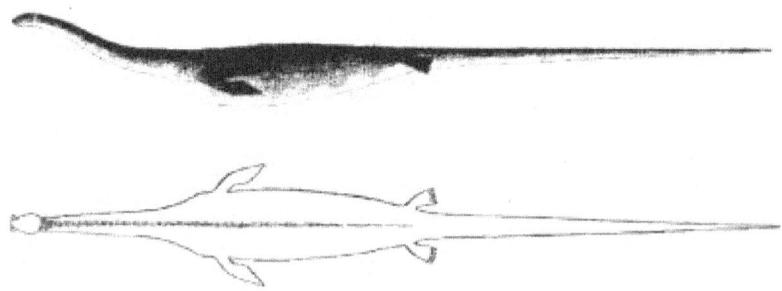

Figure 21: According to A.C. Oudemans, the Megophias megophias can adequately explain sea serpent legends.

Author Dallas Turner, who has written a fictional cryptid series, including *Wake of the Lake Monster,* has researched the topic extensively. Turner believes that an ancestor of migratory seals is responsible for many lake monster/sea serpent sightings as they follow their food supply. According to Turner, legends have their root in something—a seal-like creature could explain a great many aquatic cryptid reports.

As fascinating as it is to ponder the existence of undiscovered marine mammals, there are many examples of marine mammals such as seals and manatees being misidentified in their home waters. As the creatures dive, they tend to resemble the famous "humps" of sea serpent descriptions. When these animals are in groups feeding, they can create a "multi-humped" appearance and create wakes on the water.

What if the Caribbean Monk Seal is Not Extinct?

If perchance a small, surviving population of Caribbean monk seals exist, then many sea serpent sightings in the Caribbean are explainable. Moreover, some sightings as far north as Florida could be attributed to this remnant population as well.

Though officially declared extinct in 2008, and last confirmed to be alive in 1952—scientists readily admit that there were probably seals that lived well into the 1970s. Many attempts were made to locate surviving seals; key among these efforts were aerial surveys conducted over the range of the seals. Nothing was found. Still, though, I wonder: can we be absolutely certain that none remain? After all, trying to locate a seal, or at best a small number of seals, over such a vast area is tantamount to finding the proverbial needle in a haystack. It is not easy to know exactly when a species ceases to exist, or if this has occurred at all.

Australia's legendary Tasmanian tiger is thought to have gone extinct in 1936. As recently as 2014, however, there have been reported sightings. Over the decades, sightings have been such a regular occurrence that History's *MonsterQuest* investigated the phenomenon and aired an episode in 2009. In the same way that some believe that the Tasmanian tiger still exists, there are those who believe the Caribbean monk seal may still be alive as well. There may be evidence, albeit anecdotal, to back up the claims.

In 1997, fisherman from Haitian and Jamaican villages were interviewed; there were 93 participants. Of the 93, 16 claimed to have seen at least one Caribbean monk seal during the last two years.[1] To this day, divers and fisherman report seeing a Caribbean monk seal from time to time. Some are skeptical of the claims, and attribute the sightings to hooded seals. There are confirmed sightings of hooded seals as far south as Puerto Rico and the Virgin Islands. As for me, I tend to believe native fishermen who are on the water every day over the opinions of skeptics who are *certain* that the fishermen are mistaken.

Even if there is a remnant population of Caribbean monk seals, the odds are against them; it is my fear that they will not last much longer. Unfortunately, their relatives, Hawaiian monk seals and Mediterranean monk seals, are declining in their numbers. Hopefully, mankind will take the initiative and protect these animals so they do not suffer the same fate as their Caribbean cousins.

Strange Encounters during the Voyages of Columbus

The intrepid Italian explorer, Christopher Columbus, set foot on the shores of the New World in October of 1492. Columbus would also complete three other voyages to the New World under the auspices of the Spanish crown. The monarchs in Spain had a simple agenda—the voyages were funded in order to set up trade routes and permanent colonies.

Whether or not Columbus actually *discovered* the New World is a matter of debate; in my mind, the issue is far from settled. Pre-Columbian exploration of the Americas certainly seems to have taken place; a number of seafaring peoples are thought to have reached the New World long ago.

Some place the Polynesians in South America in the remote past; evidence seems to suggest that the Chinese may have set foot in modern-day California long before Columbus landed in the Bahamas. We know that the rugged, Icelandic explorer Leif Erikson reached North America centuries before Columbus set sail. Some believe that the Norse may have travelled as far south as present-day Martha's Vineyard, Massachusetts. Before the Norse—an astonishing 500 years earlier—the Irish are thought to have reached North America on their leather covered wooden boats. Going even further back, thousands of years—in the heart of the Bronze Age—evidence suggests that copper mining occurred in the Great Lakes region. Who were these miners? Some believe the Minoans! The theories concerning the discovery of the New World and pre-Columbian exploration could make up an entire book—or series of books—on its own.

Of course, European contact, set in motion by Columbus, had an extraordinary, irreversible, and even a regrettable impact upon the indigenous peoples, fauna, and ecosystems of the New World. Earlier, we discussed the Caribbean monk seal and its demise. Unfortunately, the road to extinction began during the second voyage of Columbus. This is when Columbus ordered eight Caribbean monk seals to be killed and butchered to feed his men—the rest is history.

Strange Occurrences and Strange Creatures

The expeditions that Columbus led to the New World had their share of strange events. Reports of strange animals, mermaids, and peculiar aerial phenomenon have been recorded.

Mermaid sightings have long been a staple of maritime tales. Famed explorer Henry Hudson recorded a mermaid sighting that occurred in the Arctic in his ship log. While searching a second time for a northeastern passage, two of Hudson's crewmen saw a mermaid. Like Hudson's crew members, Christopher Columbus claimed to see mermaids as well. The incident occurred on January 9, 1493, when Columbus saw three mermaids come to the surface. Columbus wrote that the mermaids did not possess the beauty so often attributed to them. Interestingly, it has been said that Columbus had seen mermaids before reaching the New World when sailing off the coast of Africa.

Today, it has been decided that Columbus saw manatees rather than mermaids. This would definitely explain his disappointment with their physical appearance, and how they did not live up to their reputation or their depictions in paintings. One has to wonder though— although it is easy to dismiss the existence of a therianthrope such as a mermaid, did Columbus really mistake manatees for mermaids? If so, how? *They look nothing alike!*

The strange creatures that Columbus encountered in the New World were not limited to mermaids/manatees. In 1492, two of Columbus' men killed strange serpents measuring up to five feet in length. The snakes might not have been unusual at all—only weird to Europeans unfamiliar with the fauna of the tropics in the New World. Likewise, an *ape-faced cat* was captured in present-day Costa Rica during the fourth voyage. It is hard to know exactly what this creature was, but perhaps for Costa Rica, it was not unusual at all. We will never know.

A behemoth turtle of sorts was spotted by Columbus and his crew off the coast of Hispaniola, modern-day Haiti and the Dominican Republic. Dubbed the Father of all the Turtles, this gargantuan turtle was said to be the size of a whale. Similar reports of these massive beasts have occurred as far north as Nova Scotia and south to the Columbian coast. A world away, in Indonesia, off the coast of Sumatra, the Father of all the Turtles is also said to dwell. It is firmly established in local maritime legends.

Perhaps more unusual than the strange animals Columbus encountered is an aerial phenomenon known as *orbs*. The sighting occurred at night on his first voyage just before landfall. In his journal, Columbus described the strange lights as: "A small wax candle that rose and lifted up." Some have proposed that Columbus was seeing light from a torch on land nearby. Others believe that he was seeing some sort of bioluminescence. This may be. However, Columbus was obviously a seasoned sailor; I tend to believe that he would have encountered bioluminescence in the water before—and not be fooled by it. Certainly, he had seen torches on the land before; it seems unlikely, at least to me, that torches would've tricked Columbus. The way in which he describes the orbs seems as though he is seeing something in the air. I have to wonder—the account is eerily similar to orbs that are frequently associated with modern-day UFO reports—could it be?

Chapter Four: Conclusion

Some Monsters that weren't

Anytime lake monsters, or any type cryptid, is the topic of study, hoaxes are sure to come to the forefront. This is unfortunate; it can be hard to understand what motivates people who perpetrate hoaxes. The cryptid enthusiast must always be vigilant and keep a watchful eye for those who would like to make fools of believers.

On the North American continent, there are a few "creatures" that come to mind that are probably nothing more than hoaxes. Nebraska's only lake monster, the Alkali Monster is probably nothing more than tall tales that became embedded in the local folklore. The bizarre Oklahoma Octopus, blamed for drowning deaths in three manmade lakes, is probably another hoax. The killer octopus owes its fame to Animal Planet's *Lost Tapes*; the *Lost Tapes* episode seemed to borrow heavily from a Stephen King short story. Even a creature with over 600 documented sightings, in addition to photographs, video, and audio recordings, has been the target of pranksters. The Lake Champlain Monster, or Champ, was the victim of outlandish newspaper reports in the 1800s. Sensational, and unfortunately, sometimes false stories were fairly common back in the day as a means of boosting readership.

Like their neighbors to the north, Central and South America, Mexico, and the Caribbean are not immune from hoaxes. It could be said that the creature Chan, which was covered earlier in this book is a hoax. After all, there is little evidence for the existence of the creature and the photographic evidence is suspect at best. The Panama Monster and the creature from the San Miguel Lagoon could fit the bill as well. However, there are some reports, which, at their worst, are definite hoaxes; at best, they are cases of mistaken identity. We shall examine a few.

The Monster of Lake Fagua

A bizarre winged creature, best described as a harpy, supposedly terrorized the population surrounding a Chilean lake in the late 1700s. The frightening creature allegedly preyed upon local livestock in the dead of night. The monster had two tails. One tail was pointed with a sharp tip; the creature used this tail to spear its victims. The other tail was used to snatch its prey; this tail had rings or suckers—possibly something similar to the tentacles of an octopus. The two-tailed beast was 11 feet in length. It had long, droopy ears that were similar to a donkey and a human face. The ghastly brute had large horns protruding from its head and a horse-like mane.[1]

In 1784, an article in *Courier de L' Europe* claimed that this creature had been captured and was going to be put on display in Europe.[2] This, of course, never happened. In fact, the creature never existed—it was a caricature of Queen Marie Antoinette. In 1784, the seeds of revolution were taking root in France. The royal family, with their excesses, were hated by the struggling people. The Monster of Lake Fagua, rather than being a real creature, was a frustrated population's way of mocking the nobility.[3]

Today, the Bibliothèque Nationale de France, France's national library, located in Paris, holds a broadsheet with mention of the winged monster.[4]

A Plesiosaur Carcass?

In 1927, reports began to emerge of the discovery of a plesiosaur carcass on the banks of Lago Fagnano, a long, narrow, deep lake that straddles Chile and Argentina on Tierra del Fuego Island.

Lake Fagnano had long been rumored to hold some sort of strange creature; in fact, the creature was even given a name—Fañanito. As is so often the case, the carcass reports turned out to be completely false; the remains of a plesiosaur were not found on Tierra del Fuego Island.[5]

Today, it is widely believed that lake monster sightings in Lake Fagnano are caused by beavers. Beavers were introduced to the lake in the late 1940s. It is argued that the movements of beavers, especially groups of beavers, closely mimic the long-necked appearance and undulating body common among lake monster reports. This is a reasonable hypothesis, and when taken with the plesiosaur carcass hoax, it would appear that Lake Fagnano is void of an actual lake monster. Still, though, how do you explain sightings in the lake before the hoax and before beavers were introduced?

The Tecolutla Monster

In early 1969, the town of Tecolutla, in Veracruz, Mexico, was firmly in the grip of monster hysteria after a strange, unrecognizable carcass washed upon a beach. The badly decomposed corpse, recovered by a group of farmers who happened upon it one night, was 72 feet long. According to some reports, it weighed over 24 tons; other reports have the monster tipping the scales at 35 tons or more.

The story of the strange carcass really gets weird.

The farmers who discovered the corpse kept it hidden for about a week, but eventually informed the mayor. The mayor, Caesar Guerrero, believed the corpse was a downed plane and organized a rescue party. However, this was no plane—it was a mass of rotting flesh that was partially buried. The body was serpentine in shape and was covered in armor and also had wool. The creature had horns and a beak.[6]

Another weird turn in the tale—there were fishermen who claimed that the beast was still alive when they encountered it; it died a short time later.[7]

Mayor Guerrero asked for help in identifying the creature. He reached out to biologists from the fish and biology station in Tampico. Scientists were unable to identify the animal at first; it had been too disfigured.[8] Eventually, though, the creature was confirmed to be a whale.

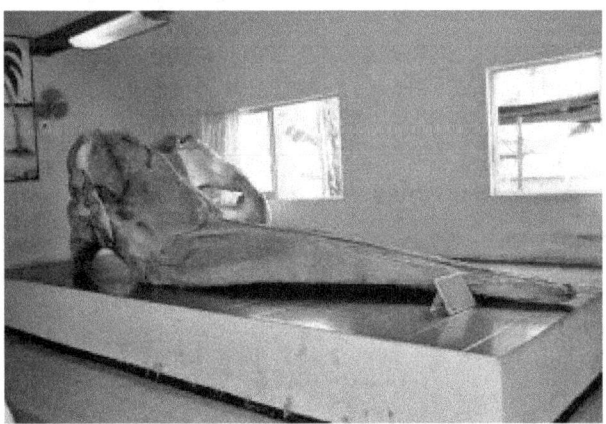

Figure 22: Skull from the Tecolutla Monster in the Marine Museum. By AlejandroLinaresGarcia - Own work, CC BY-SA 3.0, https://commons.wikimedia.org/w/index.php?curid=18857633

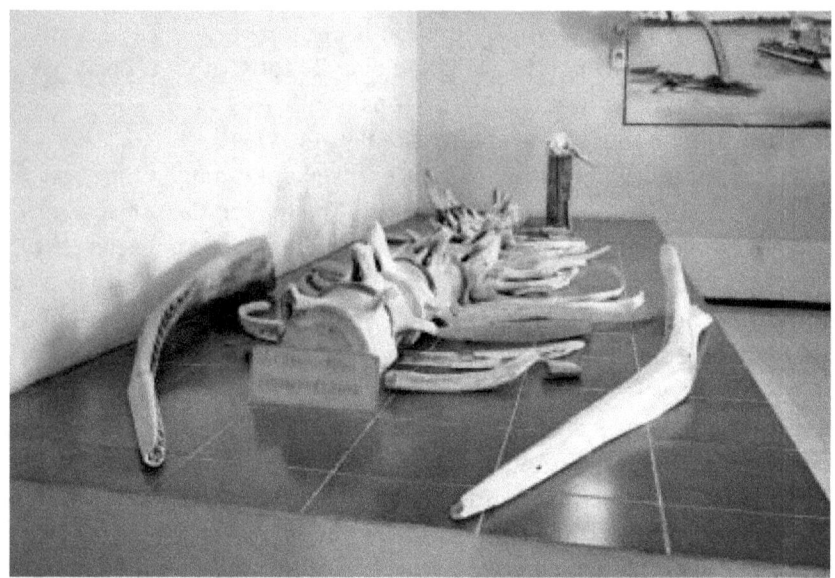

Figure 23: Ribs and vertebrae from the Tecolutla Monster. By AlejandroLinaresGarcia - Own work, CC BY-SA 3.0, https://commons.wikimedia.org/w/index.php?curid=18857596:

Though nothing came of it, and it ended up being nothing extraordinary, the Tecolutla Monster created quite a stir in the seaside community. After scientists studied the body, the mayor would not allow it to be buried; rather, he ordered it to be left as a tourist attraction. Today, its bones are on display in the town's marine museum.

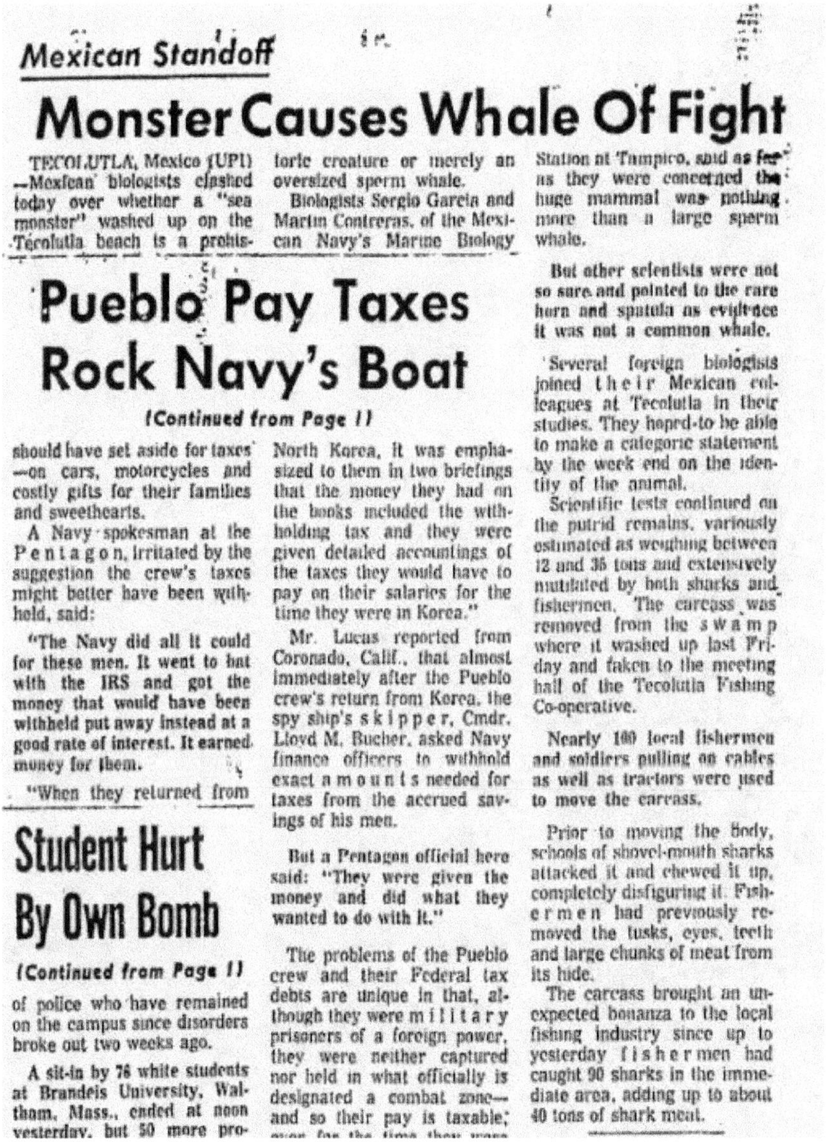

Mexican Standoff

Monster Causes Whale Of Fight

TECOLUTLA, Mexico (UPI) —Mexican biologists clashed today over whether a "sea monster" washed up on the Tecolutla beach is a prehistoric creature or merely an oversized sperm whale.

Biologists Sergio Garcia and Martin Contreras, of the Mexican Navy's Marine Biology Station at Tampico, said as far as they were concerned the huge mammal was nothing more than a large sperm whale.

But other scientists were not so sure and pointed to the rare horn and spatula as evidence it was not a common whale.

Several foreign biologists joined their Mexican colleagues at Tecolutla in their studies. They hoped to be able to make a categoric statement by the week end on the identity of the animal.

Scientific tests continued on the putrid remains, variously estimated as weighing between 12 and 35 tons and extensively mutilated by both sharks and fishermen. The carcass was removed from the swamp where it washed up last Friday and taken to the meeting hall of the Tecolutla Fishing Co-operative.

Nearly 100 local fishermen and soldiers pulling on cables as well as tractors were used to move the carcass.

Prior to moving the body, schools of shovel-mouth sharks attacked it and chewed it up, completely disfiguring it. Fishermen had previously removed the tusks, eyes, teeth and large chunks of meat from its hide.

The carcass brought an unexpected bonanza to the local fishing industry since up to yesterday fishermen had caught 90 sharks in the immediate area, adding up to about 40 tons of shark meat.

Pueblo Pay Taxes Rock Navy's Boat

(Continued from Page 1)

should have set aside for taxes —on cars, motorcycles and costly gifts for their families and sweethearts.

A Navy spokesman at the Pentagon, irritated by the suggestion the crew's taxes might better have been withheld, said:

"The Navy did all it could for these men. It went to bat with the IRS and got the money that would have been withheld put away instead at a good rate of interest. It earned money for them.

"When they returned from North Korea, it was emphasized to them in two briefings that the money they had on the books included the withholding tax and they were given detailed accountings of the taxes they would have to pay on their salaries for the time they were in Korea."

Mr. Lucas reported from Coronado, Calif., that almost immediately after the Pueblo crew's return from Korea, the spy ship's skipper, Cmdr. Lloyd M. Bucher, asked Navy finance officers to withhold exact amounts needed for taxes from the accrued savings of his men.

But a Pentagon official here said: "They were given the money and did what they wanted to do with it."

The problems of the Pueblo crew and their Federal tax debts are unique in that, although they were military prisoners of a foreign power, they were neither captured nor held in what officially is designated a combat zone— and so their pay is taxable, even for the time they were

Student Hurt By Own Bomb

(Continued from Page 1)

of police who have remained on the campus since disorders broke out two weeks ago.

A sit-in by 76 white students at Brandeis University, Waltham, Mass., ended at noon yesterday, but 50 more pro-

Figure 24: An article that appeared in the Pittsburg Press on March 7, 1969.

Science Sniffs, Says 'Monster' Just A Whale

TECOLUTLA, Mexico (UPI) —The "Monster of Tecolutla" is just a rare type of whale, scientists say.

"It is our conclusion that this specimen is a whale of the type known to us a rorqual," a seven-man commission of scientists concluded in a report completed Sunday.

The Rorqual is also known as the finback whale because of its large bony dorsal fin—one of the characteristics that led to the belief it was a "monster sea creature" never seen before by man.

"This specimen has been dead for at least a month," the scientists said.

The c a r c a s s was being buried at the beach and one onlooker said "the smell is enormous—just stunning."

The scientists ordered the whale buried for three months and said they would exhume its skeleton then for the National Maritime Science Study Center. But Tecolutla Mayor Cosur Guerrero said local authorities would keep it here as a tourist attraction.

Figure 25: This article appeared in the Pittsburg Press on March 11, 1969.

Some Final Observations

When I set out to write this book, I had many preconceived ideas about the water monster phenomenon south of the border. In my first work, *People are Seeing Something: A Survey of Lake Monsters in the United States and Canada,* I could find definite similarities between many of the creatures that I covered. Additionally, the lakes in which these creatures dwell also share many of the same characteristics. Of course, this is not true in all cases, but particularly in the northern United States and Canada, there seemed to be a definite correlation between glacial lakes and creatures similar to the Loch Ness Monster. Writing this book has reinforced my position.

While the cold, glacial lakes of Canada and the United States seem to hold a number of quintessential "sea serpents," monsters in the waters of Central and South America, the Caribbean, and Mexico seem to fall under several categories:

- Giant snakes, reminiscent of the "mythical" giant anaconda.
- Massive fish—possibly large enough to prey on humans.
- Animals that are best described as "living dinosaurs."
- "Water Tigers."
- Mythical creatures.

Typical Lake Monsters

It is not until you arrive at the lakes high in the Andes, or those of the Patagonia region of Chile and Argentina, at the tip, or cone of the South American Continent, that *typical* lake monsters (those who resemble the Loch Ness Monster, Champ, and the Ogopogo) are seen with any regularity.

Like Canada and the northern United States, Patagonia was also covered in an immense ice sheet in the prehistoric past. The ice reached its peak about 17,000 years ago. Today, an aerial view of the landscape testifies to an icy past; gouges in the earth, now filled with water, speak to a tumultuous time in prior ages. What is true in North America is also true in South America—there is a definite link between glacial lakes and *typical* lake monster reports. It seems that somehow, some sort of large, marine reptiles became trapped in glacial lakes, perhaps after meltwater receded at the conclusion of the last ice age, and established small, breeding colonies in these lakes at various locations throughout the world. I know it sounds crazy, and I'm not asking you to believe it—but the link between glacial lakes and lake monsters cannot be denied.

The Amazon

To anyone with an open mind, the Amazon Rainforest, with its seemingly never-ending tree canopy and its myriad of waterways, could hold nearly any creature—known or unknown. There is probably not a better place on earth for cryptids to dwell. Would it really be that big of a surprise if some sort of holdover from the age of the dinosaurs was alive in the swamps and jungles of Amazonia?

We know that giant snakes and gargantuan fish are alive and well in the Amazon; the climate and habitat are conducive to these animals being able to reach colossal proportions. But could there be fish and snakes that are much larger than we what we already know? If there are species of catfish that have been verified to tip the scales at around 400 pounds, is it unreasonable to believe that there could be outliers who weigh closer to 1,000 pounds—large enough to eat a man?

Myths

The Caribbean and Central and South America are rich in folklore and legends. There are many legends of creatures that are only alive in myths and stories. Some of these have been discussed in this book. What are these ancient legends trying to tell us and how did they originate?

Giant Sharks

It might be possible to add a category for sea creatures south of the border as well. The Caribbean is home to several sea monsters including a large, segmented worm referred to as "the thing;" a giant octopus, reminiscent of the legendary Kraken; and truly monstrous sharks. Across the continent, in the Gulf of California, giant sharks are said to exist as well.

What can only be described as a monster was caught by Cuban fisherman in 1945; dubbed "el Monstruo de Cojimar," the massive great white measured 21 feet in length and weighed a whopping 7,000 pounds! What was once thought of as a "fish story," due to the fact that great whites normally range between 11-16 feet in length, was confirmed to be true in 2015 when a documentary crew working for the *Discovery Channel* went to Cuba to investigate the legend.[1]

The coral reefs off of the coast of Cuba are prime habitat for populations of large sharks. Many believe that it is not a question of if, but of when, another monster—a record-setting shark will be discovered.

Sharks that dwarf "el Monstruo de Cojimar," may be lurking in the depths of the Sea of Cortez (also known as the Gulf of California). Colossal sharks, collectively known as the Black Demon, have been spotted that measure an incredible 60 feet in length and weigh tens of thousands of pounds. This has led many to speculate that this is either a new, or rather, an uncategorized species of shark, or—and perhaps more disturbing—a remnant population of Megalodon sharks.

Could the apex predator, the prehistoric Megalodon be alive today? Scientists are quick to say no. But, does the possibility exist? The Sea of Cortez reaches depths exceeding 9,800 feet in spots; what kind of mysterious creatures could be lurking in this abyss?

In Closing

I hope that you have enjoyed reading this book. If you liked reading it half as much as I enjoyed writing it, then I have done my job. I come away from this book with firmer convictions than ever before. I truly believe that almost *anything* could be living in the remote regions and deep waters south of the border. When my guide in Peru, Chamo, told me that the jungle has secrets, I believe him. I, now, more than ever, believe we do not know what goes on inside the jungle, and we do not know everything that lives there. I am convinced more than ever that we don't know as much as we would like to think—and we understand even less.

Bibliography

"¿Ahora Huechulito?" Bariloche 2000. May 22, 2009. Accessed July 13, 2016.
http://bariloche2000.com/noticias/leer/ahora-huechulito/38989.

"The Ahuizotl." The Aztecs at Mexicolore. Accessed May 15, 2016.
http://www.mexicolore.co.uk/aztecs/aztefacts/ahuizotl.

Alexander, Hartley Burr. *The Mythology of All Races.* Edited by Louis Herbert Gray and George Foot Moore. Vol. XI. Latin America. Boston: Marshall Jones Company, 1920. Accessed April 24, 2016. Google Books.

"Aliens and Temples of Gold." *Ancient Aliens.* 2011. New York, NY: History.

"Ancient Temple Found under Lake Titicaca." BBC News. August 23, 2000. Accessed April 17, 2016.
http://news.bbc.co.uk/2/hi/americas/892616.stm.

The Aquarist and Pondkeeper. Cornell University. Volumes 34–35, 1969, p182.
https://books.google.com/books?id=AztMAAAAYAAJ.

Bassett, Fletcher S. "The Gods, Saints, and Demons of the Sea: Nick and Davey Jones, the Virgin." In *Legends and Superstitions of the Sea and of Sailors: In All Lands and at All Times*, 93. Chicago: Belford, Clarke, & Co., 1885.

Blakley, Julie. "Top 10 Shark Infested Beaches in the World." BootsnAll Travel Articles. September 2, 2015. Accessed March 13, 2016. http://www.bootsnall.com/articles/08-10/10-most-shark-infested-beaches-world.html.

"Blue Holes - Lairs of the Lusca." Search of Life. January 29, 2014. Accessed February 16, 2016.
http://searchoflife.com/blue-holes-lairs-of-the-lusca-2014-01-29.

"Body Snatcher." *River Monsters.* Produced by Patrick Keegan. 2014. New York, NY: Animal Planet.

"Bull Shark." National Geographic. Accessed March 13, 2016.
http://animals.nationalgeographic.com/animals/fish/bull-shark/.

"The Bull Sharks of Lake Nicaragua" Nicaragua.com. Accessed March 13, 2016.
http://www.nicaragua.com/blog/the-bull-sharks-of-lake-nicaragua.

"Buscarán Una Extraña Criatura En un Lago De Junín De Los Andes." Infobae. May 19, 2009. Accessed July 13, 2016. http://www.infobae.com/2009/05/19/449247-buscaran-una-extrana-criatura-un-lago-junin-los-andes/.

Calhoun, Cynthia. "What Is the Legend of El Dorado and the Gold of the Chibchas." HubPages. November 25, 2015. Accessed April 24, 2016. http://hubpages.com/travel/legend-of-el-dorado-and-the-chibchas.

"Camahueto." Fundi2 | Everything Chilean. 2012. Accessed February 22, 2016.
https://fundi2.com/2012/03/09/camahueto/.

"Camahueto." Myths and Legends from Chiloé. Accessed February 22, 2016.
http://mandradey.wix.com/myths#!en-blanco/c1sm5.

"Caribbean Monk Seal Gone Extinct From Human Causes, NOAA Confirms." ScienceDaily. June 9, 2008. Accessed February 21, 2016.

"Caribbean Monk Seal." Seal Conservation Society. Accessed February 21, 2016.

"Category Archives: Mexican Cultural Stories." Surviving Mexico. Accessed March 06, 2016.
http://survivingmexico.com/category/mexican-cultural-stories/.

Cepeda, Karen Sachica, and Abde Rahman El Gamal. "Cage Culture of Rainbow Trout in Lake Tota (Colombia)." Fish Consulting Group. January 27, 2016. Accessed May 01, 2016.
http://fishconsult.org/?p=13126.

Chisholm, C., M.D. *An Essay on the Malignant Pestilential Fever.* Vol. II. London: F. Gillet, 1801. Accessed February 23, 2016. Google Books.

Chorvinsky, Mark. "NAHUELITO, PATAGONIAN LAKE MONSTER." Strangemag.com. Accessed March 03, 2016.

Christenson, Allen J. *Art and Society in a Highland Maya Community: The Altarpiece of Santiago Atitlán.* Austin, TX: University of Texas Press, 2001.

Clark, Leonard. *The Rivers Ran East.* New York: Funk & Wagnalls, 1953.

"Diplodocus in the Amazon." Colonel Fawcett's Dinosaur. Accessed March 01, 2016. http://www.fawcettadventure.com/colonel_fawcett's_dinosaur.html.

Drinnon, Dale A. "'Little Gold Sea Monster' No Longer Alone." Frontiers of Zoology. May 4, 2012. Accessed August 13, 2016. http://frontiersofzoology.blogspot.com/2012/05/little-gold-sea-monster-no-longer-alone.html.

Cohen, Daniel. *Monsters, Giants, and Little Men from Mars: An Unnatural History of the Americas.* Garden City, NY: Doubleday, 1975.

Coppens, Phillip. "Jurassic Library." Phillip Coppens. Accessed March 29, 2016. http://philipcoppens.com/jurassiclibrary.html.

Dinsdale, Tim. *The Leviathans.* London: Routledge & K. Paul, 1966.

"Divers Probe Mayan Ruins Submerged in Guatemala Lake." Reuters. October 30, 2009. Accessed March 13, 2016. http://www.reuters.com/article/us-guatemala-archaeology-idUSTRE59T4P120091030.

Eberhart, George M. *Mysterious Creatures: A Guide to Cryptozoology.* Santa Barbara, CA: ABC-CLIO, 2002.

"El Cuero." Cryptid Wiki. Accessed March 06, 2016. http://cryptidz.wikia.com/wiki/El_Cuero.

Farra, Leonard. "The El Dorado - ET Link - World Mysteries Blog." World Mysteries Blog. July 06, 2013. Accessed April 24, 2016. http://blog.world-mysteries.com/mystic-places/the-el-dorado-et-link/.

Fawcett, Percy Harrison. *Exploration Fawcett; Arranged from His Manuscripts, Letters, Log-books, and Records.* London: Hutchinson, 1953.

Foer, Joshua. "Giant Anacondas Lurk in This Peruvian Nature Reserve, or so Everyone Says." Slate Magazine. February 17, 2011. Accessed June 07, 2016. http://www.slate.com/articles/life/world_of_wonders/2011/02/on_the_trail_of_a_40foot_anaconda.html.

G., Jose Baez. "The Monster of Lake Tota." HIRARA: 'WHERE THE WORDS' October 21, 2013. Accessed May 01, 2016. https://josebaezg.wordpress.com/2013/10/21/el-monstruo-del-lago-de-tota/.

"Giant Catfish' Attacks Perkins Boy." NewsOK.com. August 16, 1985. Accessed July 24, 2016. http://newsok.com/article/2118087.

"Giant 'jiboia' Snake in Brazil." Forgetomori. April 29, 2008. Accessed June 07, 2016 http://forgetomori.com/2008/criptozoology/giant-jiboia-snake-in-brazil/.

Gibbons, William J. "In Search of the Congo Dinosaur." Impact, July 2002, i-iv.

"Gold, Flesh of the Gods." Ancient Astronauts. December 1, 2012. Accessed April 24, 2016. http://the-ancient-astronauts.blogspot.com/2012/12/gold-flesh-of-gods.html.

"Green Anacondas, Green Anaconda Pictures, Green Anaconda Facts - National Geographic." National Geographic. Accessed February 11, 2016.

Hapgood, Charles, and David Hatcher Childress. *Mystery in Acambaro.* Kempton, IL: Adventures Unlimited Press, 2000.

Hebblethwaite, Cordelia. "The Hunt for Mokele-mbembe: Congo's Loch Ness Monster." BBC News. December 28, 2011. Accessed March 29, 2016. http://www.bbc.com/news/magazine-16306902.

Hemming, John. "The Draining of Lake Guatavita." *South American Explorers*, August 1981, 24-26.

Heuvelmans, Bernard. Translated by Richard Garnett. In *On the Track of Unknown Animals*, 3rd ed. New York: Rutledge, 2014.

Ho, Oliver. *Mysteries Unwrapped: Mutants and Monsters.* New York: Sterling, 2008.

Hogan, Katie. "Glyryvilu." Flowers in Mud. February 10, 2016. Accessed June 08, 2016. http://www.flowersinmud.com/glyryvilu/.

Holloway, April. "Do the Ica Stones Prove That Mankind Coexisted with Dinosaurs and Had Advanced Technology?" Ancient Origins. March 10, 2014. Accessed March 29, 2016. http://www.ancient-origins.net/unexplained-phenomena/do-ica-stones-prove-mankind-coexisted-dinosaurs-advanced-technology-098989?nopaging=1.

"Hungarian Lake Catfish Attacks Fisherman." UPI. August 5, 2009.

"Iara Mermaid in Mythology." Real Mermaids. Accessed February 23, 2016.
  http://www.realmermaids.net/mermaid-legends/iara-mermaid/

Johnson, Ben. "The Kelpie." Historic UK. Accessed March 30, 2016. http://www.historic-
  uk.com/CultureUK/The-Kelpie/.

Keate, George. "Nessie Hunter Solves Monster Mystery." The Times. July 16, 2015. Accessed July
  24, 2016. http://www.thetimes.co.uk/tto/environment/wildlife/article4499438.ece.

Keel, John A. The Complete Guide to Mysterious Beings. New York: Doubleday, 1994.

"Kids Kill Panama 'Montauk Monster' by Lake." Perth Now. September 18, 2009. Accessed May
  12, 2016. http://www.perthnow.com.au/news/world/kids-kill-panama-montauk-monster-
  by-lake/story-e6frg1p3-1225776476121.

Kirk, John. In the Domain of the Lake Monsters. Toronto: Key Porter Books, 1998.

"Lake Titicaca Reveals More Ancient Underwater Secrets." MessageToEagle.com. October 11,
  2013. Accessed April 17, 2016.
  http://www.messagetoeagle.com/laketiticacarelics.php#.VxOQVfkrLIV.

"Lake Tota, Colombia Vacation Info." Lakelubbers. Accessed May 01, 2016.
  http://www.lakelubbers.com/lake-tota-2228/.

Lehmann, Pablo, Lucas J. Schvambach, and Roberto E. Reis. A New Species of the Armored Catfish
  Parotocinclus (Loricariidae: Hypoptopmatinae), from the Amazon Basin in Columbia. PDF.
  Neotropical Ichthyology, 2015.

"Lisburn Men Find Giant Snake in the Amazon." Ulster Star. June 4, 2009. Accessed June 07,
  2016. http://www.lisburntoday.co.uk/news/lisburn-news/lisburn-men-find-giant-snake-in-
  the-amazon-1-1642677.

MacDonald, Christine. "Green Going Gone: The Tragic Deforestation of the Chaco." Rolling Stone.
  July 28, 2014. Accessed July 24, 2016. http://www.rollingstone.com/culture/news/green-
  going-gone-the-tragic-deforestation-of-the-chaco-20140728.

Mackal, Roy P. "Biochemical Analyses of Preserved Octopus giganteus Tissue." Cryptozoology,
  1986. 55–62

"Mermaids from South America." Tales of Faerie. June 17, 2015. Accessed February 23, 2016.
  http://talesoffaerie.blogspot.com/2015/06/mermaids-from-south-america.html

"The Minhocoa." Knowledge 1 (May 26, 1882): 302. Accessed August 1, 2016. Google.

"Missing Link – Gone AWOL." Blather. November 07, 1997. Accessed March 06, 2016.
  http://www.blather.net/theblather/1997/11/missing_link_gone_awol/.

Mkassa2. "MonsterQuest Giant Killer Fish - National Geographic Documentary." YouTube. August
  17, 2014. Accessed July 24, 2016. http://www.youtube.com/watch?v=D6vd4m3j-bg.

"Mokele-mbembe Expedition 2015." YouTube. August 27, 2014. Accessed March 29, 2016.
  https://www.youtube.com/watch?v=lAlQ2tt5074.

"Monster Boa Size of Two Buses Reported by Terrified Village." DrudgeReportArchives.com.
  August 20, 1997. Accessed June 07, 2016.
  http://www.drudgereportarchives.com/dsp/specialReports_pc_carden_detail.htm?reportI
  D={D94065F2-D484-4E15-BC50-A69724F52803}.

Originally appeared as a Reuters Wire Service Report.

Morphy, Rob. "EL CUERO: (ARGENTINA - CHILI) - Cryptopia - Exploring the Hidden World."
  Cryptopia. December 15, 2009. Accessed March 06, 2016.

"Moustruo En Neuquen! El 'Huechulito'" Taringa. Accessed July 13, 2016.
  http://www.taringa.net/posts/noticias/2605889/Moustruo-en-neuquen-el-
  Huechulito.html.

Mustafa, Sam. "The Myth of Nahuelito: A Monstrous Symbol of Argentina." The Argentina
  Independent. November 25, 2010. Accessed March 03, 2016.

"Mystery Monster." The Dispatch (Lexington), August 23, 1971.

Naish, Darren. "Whatever Happened to the Tecolutla Monster?" Tetrapod Zoology. July 10, 2008.
  Accessed August 01, 2016.
  http://scienceblogs.com/tetrapodzoology/2008/07/10/tecolutla-monster-carcass/.

"New 'Jaguar' Catfish Species Found in Amazon." LiveScience. March 2, 2011. Accessed July 24,
  2016. http://www.livescience.com/30196-new-species-catfish-amazon-river.html.

"New 'Montauk Monster' Spotted in Panama." The Telegraph. September 17, 2009. Accessed May 12, 2016. http://www.telegraph.co.uk/news/worldnews/centralamericaandthecaribbean/panama/6 201333/New-Montauk-Monster-spotted-in-Panama.html.

Newton, Michael. *Hidden Animals: A Field Guide to Batsquatch, Chupacabra, and Other Elusive Creatures*. Santa Barbara, CA: Greenwood Press, 2009.

"Old and New Mermaids, Superstitions, Etc." *Asiatic Journal*, January 1823, 51-52. Accessed February 23, 2016. Google Books.

Parker, Chris. "Eyewitness Accounts -Do Dinosaurs Still Exist? Page 8." S8int.com. Accessed April 17, 2016. http://s8int.com/eyewit8.html.

"Piraiba Fresh Water Monsters." Bass Fishing Gurus. 2015. Accessed July 24, 2016. http://www.bassfishing-gurus.com/piraiba-fresh-water-monsters/.

Porteous, Alexander. "Forest Folklore, Mythology, and Romance." In *The Lore of the Forest*, 146. New York: Cosimo, 2005.

Posse, Eugenia Villa. *Mitos Y Leyedas De Columbia*. Vol. II. Quito: Diego De Atienz a Y Av. Améric a, 1993.

Patton, Don. "The Dinosaur Figurines of Acambaro, Mexico." http://www.bible.ca/tracks/tracks-acambaro.htm. Accessed June 13, 2016.

Putnam, George Palmer. *The Southland of North America: Ramblings and Observations in Central America during the Year 1912*. New York: Knickerbocker Press, 1914. Accessed April 24, 2016. Google Books.

Rose, Carol. *Giants, Monsters, and Dragons: An Encyclopedia of Folklore, Legend, and Myth*. New York: W.W. Norton & Company, 2000.

Ross, Sara. "The Ica Stones." Pseudoarchaeology Research Archive. May 21, 2007. Accessed March 29, 2016. http://pseudoarchaeology.org/b03-ross.html.

Roth, Aaron. "The Monster of Lake Atitlan." Aaron Roth Stories and Monthly Newsletters from Latin America. January 17, 2011. Accessed March 13, 2016. http://www.aaronroth.net/2011/01/17/the-monster-of-lake-atitlan/.

Saavedra, Mario Masvidal. "The Creature from the San Miguel Lagoon." OnCuba. May 24, 2012. Accessed February 15, 2016. http://oncubamagazine.com/magazine-articles/creature-san-miguel lagoon/.

San Martin, Rodrigo Valenzuela. "Lake Tota Monster." Críptidos Y Fantasía. July 18, 2014. Accessed May 01, 2016. http://criptidosyfantasia.blogspot.com/2014/07/el-monstruo-del-lago-de-tota-un.html.

Seaburn, Paul. "Ahuizotl: Aztec Man-Eating Monster and Secret to Longevity." Mysterious Universe. January 18, 2015. Accessed May 15, 2016. http://mysteriousuniverse.org/2015/01/ahuizotl-aztec-man-eating-monster-and-secret-to-longevity/.

Shuker, Karl. "Giant Anacondas and Other Super-sized Cryptozoological Snakes." ShukerNature. September 20, 2013. Accessed June 07, 2016. http://karlshuker.blogspot.com/2013/09/giant-anacondas-and-other-super-sized.html.

Shuker, Karl. "Sachamama - A Snake in a Shell?" ShukerNature. October 3, 2010. Accessed June 07, 2016. http://karlshuker.blogspot.com/2010/10/sachamama-snake-in-shell.html.

Shuker, Karl. "ShukerNature's Top Ten Living Dinosaurs of Cryptozoology." ShukerNature. January 22, 2013. Accessed March 01, 2016.

Sitchin, Zecharia. *The Lost Realms*. Santa Fe, NM: Bear, 1990.

Stanfield, M. P., and I. L. Boyd. "Circumstantial Evidence for the Presence of Monk Seals in the West Indies." *Onyx* 32, 1998.

Storm, Rory. *Monster Hunt: The Guide to Cryptozoology*. New York, NY: Sterling Pub., 2008.

"Strange & Unexplained - Dinosaurs That Are Still Alive?" Strange & Unexplained. Accessed March 01, 2016. http://www.skygaze.com/content/strange/Dinosaurs.shtml.

Swancer, Brent. "The Mysterious Blue Holes of the Bahamas." Mysterious Universe. June 17, 2014. Accessed February 16, 2016. http://mysteriousuniverse.org/2014/06/the-mysterious-blue-holes-of-the-bahamas/.

Swancer, Brent. "Way Out of Place Aquatic Beasts" Mysterious Universe. April 14, 2014. Accessed March 13, 2016. http://mysteriousuniverse.org/2014/04/way-out-of-place-aquatic-beasts/.

Jess Swanson. "Discovery Channel Documentary Confirms 70-Year-Old Legend of Cuban 'Monster Shark.'" Miami New Times. July 06, 2015. Accessed August 13, 2016. http://www.miaminewtimes.com/news/discovery-channel-documentary-confirms-70-year-old-legend-of-cuban-monster-shark-7731095.

Swift, Dennis. "Are the Ica Stones Fake? Skeptics under Fire." Cryptozoology Research Team. Accessed March 29, 2016. http://livingdinos.com/2011/07/are-the-ica-stones-fake-skeptics-under-fire/.

Szymanski, Greg, JD. "The Night 'The Green Blob' Destroyed Lake Atitlan." Investigative Journal. March 7, 2010. Accessed March 13, 2016. http://www.arcticbeacon.com/greg/headlines/the-night-'the-green-blob'-destroyed-lake-atitlan/.

Tanner, Dallas. "Lake Monsters." Dallas Tanner. 2011. Accessed February 21, 2016. http://trilogusmediagroup.com/dallastanner/?page_id=269.

Toorish, Jeff. "Mayans, Myths, and Monsters." Advanced Diver Magazine. Accessed March 13, 2016. http://www.advanceddivermagazine.com/articles/atitlan/atitlan.html.

Turnbull, Stephen. "Lusca Blue Hole Mystery in the Bahamas." Paranormal Studies & Investigations Canada. Accessed February 16, 2016.

Tuscaloosa News (Tuscaloosa), October 28, 1974.

"Underground Monsters." *Nature* XVIII (August 8, 1878): 389. Accessed August 1, 2016. Google.

Valle, Sabrina. "Panama 'Alien' Really a Dead, Bloated Sloth." National Geographic. November 9, 2009.

Vaudrey, Glen. "Blog 10: French Guiana." Still on the Track. March 10, 2011. Accessed June 22, 2016. http://forteanzoology.blogspot.com/2011_03_10_archive.html.

Verdes, Marcianitos. "EL MONSTRUO DEL LOCH NESS. LOS PRIMOS DE NESSIE." Marcianitos Verdes. July 20, 2008. Accessed August 13, 2016. http://marcianitosverdes.haaan.com/2008/07/el-monstruo-del-loch-ness-los-primos-de-nessie-23/.

Ward, Josh. "Bathers Beware: Giant Catfish Terrorizes Swimmers at Berlin Lake." SPIEGEL ONLINE. June 4, 2008. Accessed July 24, 2016. http://www.spiegel.de/international/zeitgeist/bathers-beware-giant-catfish-terrorizes-swimmers-at-berlin-lake-a-557636.html.

Warner, Mike. "Welcome to the Warner Amazon Expedition, Offical Site!" Big Snakes. 2011. Accessed June 07, 2016. http://www.bigsnakes.info/.

Wheeler, Virginia. "Mystery Beast Terrified Kids." The Sun. September 17, 2009. Accessed May 12, 2016. http://www.thesun.co.uk/sol/homepage/news/2642152/Mystery-beast-terrified-kids.html.

White, Laurence. "What's Stirring in the Jungle?" Belfast Telegraph. June 08, 2009. Accessed June 07, 2016. http://www.belfasttelegraph.co.uk/opinion/columnists/archive/laurence-white/whats-stirring-in-the-jungle-28482403.html.

Whittall, Austin. "Chilean Harpy." Patagonian Monsters. April 27, 2010. Accessed May 05, 2016.

Whittall, Austin. *Monsters of Patagonia: A Guide to Its Giants, Dwarves, Lake Creatures and Mythical Beasts.* Las Vegas: Zagier & Urruty Publications, 2013.

Whittall, Austin. "Setting the Stingray Hypothesis Straight." Patagonian Monsters. December 14, 2011. Accessed March 06, 2016. http://patagoniamonsters.blogspot.com/2010/04/chilean-harpy.html.

"Wihwin (Central American Water Spirit)," YouTube video, 1:01, Posted by The Ghost Watch, December 18, 2015, https://www.youtube.com/watch?v=Ve0bdbT2HIA

Winer, Lise. *Dictionary of the English/Creole of Trinidad & Tobago: On Historical Principles.* Montreal: McGill-Queen's University Press, 2009.

Yoon, Carol Kaesuk. "Amazon's Depths Yield Strange New World Of Unknown Fish." The New York Times. February 17, 1997. Accessed July 24, 2016.

http://www.nytimes.com/1997/02/18/science/amazon-s-depths-yield-strange-new-world-of-unknown-fish.html.

End Notes

Colossal Snakes of the Amazon

1. Mike Warner. "The Warner Amazon Expedition March 2009. An analysis of the evidence and theories following the discovery of Yacumama / The Black Boa." Big Snakes. 2011. Accessed June 07, 2016. http://www.bigsnakes.info/report.html.

2. Warner, "Warner Expedition Report."

3. Eberhart, *Mysterious Creatures: A Guide to Cryptozoology*, 189.

4. Karl Shuker. "Giant Anacondas and Other Super-sized Cryptozoological Snakes." ShukerNature. September 20, 2013. Accessed June 07, 2016. http://karlshuker.blogspot.com/2013/09/giant-anacondas-and-other-super-sized.html.

5. Shuker, "Giant Anacondas and Other Super-sized Cryptozoological Snakes."

6. Eberhart, *Mysterious Creatures: A Guide to Cryptozoology*, 189–190.

7. Warner, "Warner Expedition Report."

8. "Giant 'jiboia' Snake in Brazil." Forgetomori. April 29, 2008. Accessed June 07, 2016. http://forgetomori.com/2008/criptozoology/giant-jiboia-snake-in-brazil/.

9. Warner, "Warner Expedition Report."

10. Ibid.

11. Ibid.

12. Karl Shuker. "Sachamama - A Snake in a Shell?" ShukerNature. October 3, 2010. Accessed June 07, 2016. http://karlshuker.blogspot.com/2010/10/sachamama-snake-in-shell.html.

13. Laurence White. "What's Stirring in the Jungle?" Belfast Telegraph. June 08, 2009. Accessed June 07, 2016. http://www.belfasttelegraph.co.uk/opinion/columnists/archive/laurence-white/whats-stirring-in-the-jungle-28482403.html.

14. Warner, "Warner Expedition Report."

15. White, "What's Stirring in the Jungle?"

16. Warner, "Warner Expedition Report."

17. Ibid.

18. Mike Warner. "Selected items from Mike's extensive research archives." Big Snakes. 2011. Accessed June 07, 2016. http://www.bigsnakes.info/research-file.html.

19. Warner, "Selected items from Mike's extensive research archives."

Living Dinosaurs?

1. Eberhart, *Mysterious Creatures: A Guide to Cryptozoology*, 135.

2. "Strange & Unexplained - Dinosaurs That Are Still Alive?" Skygaze. Accessed March 26, 2016. http://www.skygaze.com/content/strange/Dinosaurs.shtml.

3. Eberhart, *Mysterious Creatures: A Guide to Cryptozoology*, 135.

4. Skygaze, "Strange & Unexplained - Dinosaurs That Are Still Alive?"

5. Karl Shuker. "SHUKERNATURE'S TOP TEN LIVING DINOSAURS OF CRYPTOZOOLOGY." ShukerNature. January 22, 2013. Accessed March 26, 2016. http://karlshuker.blogspot.com/2013/01/shukernatures-top-ten-living-dinosaurs.html.

6. Shuker, "SHUKERNATURE'S TOP TEN LIVING DINOSAURS OF CRYPTOZOOLOGY."

7. William J. Gibbons. "In Search of the Congo Dinosaur." *Impact*, July 2002, i-iv.

8. Gibbons, "In Search of the Congo Dinosaur."

9. Hebblethwaite, Cordelia. "The Hunt for Mokele-mbembe: Congo's Loch Ness Monster." BBC News. December 28, 2011. Accessed March 29, 2016. http://www.bbc.com/news/magazine-16306902.

10. Gibbons, "In Search of the Congo Dinosaur."

11. "Mokele-mbembe Expedition 2015." YouTube. August 27, 2014. Accessed March 29, 2016. https://www.youtube.com/watch?v=lAIQ2tt5074.

12. Gibbons, "In Search of the Congo Dinosaur."

13. Dennis Swift. "Are the Ica Stones Fake? Skeptics under Fire." Cryptozoology Research Team. Accessed March 29, 2016. http://livingdinos.com/2011/07/are-the-ica-stones-fake-skeptics-under-fire/.

14. Phillip Coppens. "Jurassic Library." Jurassic Library. Accessed March 29, 2016. http://philipcoppens.com/jurassiclibrary.html.

15. April Holloway. "Do the Ica Stones Prove That Mankind Coexisted with Dinosaurs and Had Advanced Technology?" Ancient Origins. March 10, 2014. Accessed March 29, 2016. http://www.ancient-origins.net/unexplained-phenomena/do-ica-stones-prove-mankind-coexisted-dinosaurs-advanced-technology-098989?nopaging=1.

16. Holloway, "Do the Ica Stones Prove That Mankind Coexisted with Dinosaurs and Had Advanced Technology?"

The Patagonian Plesiosaur

1. John Kirk. *In the Domain of the Lake Monsters.* (Toronto: Key Porter Books, 1998), 251.

2. Kirk, *In the Domain of the Lake Monsters,* 251.

3. Eberhart, *Mysterious Creatures: A Guide to Cryptozoology,* 365-366.

4. Kirk, *In the Domain of the Lake Monsters,* 252.

Cabralito

1. Carmen Petrini. "Cabralito: El Monstruo Del Dique Cabra Corral." El Tribuno. December 13, 2014. Accessed June 25, 2016. http://www.eltribuno.info/cabralito-el-monstruo-del-dique-cabra-corral-n481539.

2. "'Cabralito', El Nuevo Monstruo Acuático De Salta." Cronista.com. December 29, 2011. Accessed June 25, 2016. http://www.cronista.com/informaciongral/Cabralito-el-nuevo-monstruo-acuatico-de-Salta-20111229-0122.html.

3. Cronista, "'Cabralito', El Nuevo Monstruo Acuático De Salta."

4. Petrini, "Cabralito: El Monstruo Del Dique Cabra Corral."

5. Cronista, "'Cabralito', El Nuevo Monstruo Acuático De Salta."

Huechulito

1. "Moustruo En Neuquen! El 'Huechulito'" Taringa. Accessed July 13, 2016. http://www.taringa.net/posts/noticias/2605889/Moustruo-en-neuquen-el-Huechulito.html.

2. "¿Ahora Huechulito?" Bariloche 2000. May 22, 2009. Accessed July 13, 2016. http://bariloche2000.com/noticias/leer/ahora-huechulito/38989.

3. Taringa, "Moustruo En Neuquen! El 'Huechulito.'"

4. Whittall, *Monsters of Patagonia: A Guide to Its Giants, Dwarves, Lake Creatures and Mythical Beasts,* 160.

5. "Buscarán Una Extraña Criatura En un Lago De Junín De Los Andes." Infobae. May 19, 2009. Accessed July 13, 2016..

6. Whittall, *Monsters of Patagonia: A Guide to Its Giants, Dwarves, Lake Creatures and Mythical Beasts,* 161.

7. Taringa, "Moustruo En Neuquen! El 'Huechulito.'"

El Cuero

1. Rob Morphy. "EL CUERO: (ARGENTINA - CHILI) - Cryptopia - Exploring the Hidden World." Cryptopia. December 15, 2009. Accessed March 06, 2016.

The Mysterious Lake Titicaca

1. "Ancient Temple Found under Lake Titicaca." BBC News. August 23, 2000. Accessed April 17, 2016. http://news.bbc.co.uk/2/hi/americas/892616.stm.
2. Eberhart, *Mysterious Creatures: A Guide to Cryptozoology*, 290.

Lake Guatavita

1. Cynthia Calhoun. "What Is the Legend of El Dorado and the Gold of the Chibchas." HubPages. November 25, 2015. Accessed April 24, 2016. http://hubpages.com/travel/legend-of-el-dorado-and-the-chibchas.
2. John Hemming. "The Draining of Lake Guatavita." *South American Explorers*, August 1981, 24-26.

The Lake Tota Monster

1. "Lake Tota, Colombia Vacation Info." Lakelubbers. Accessed May 01, 2016. http://www.lakelubbers.com/lake-tota-2228/.
2. Karen Sachica Cepeda and Abde Rahman El Gamal. "Cage Culture of Rainbow Trout in Lake Tota (Colombia)." Fish Consulting Group. January 27, 2016. Accessed May 01, 2016. http://fishconsult.org/?p=13126.
3. Jose Baez G. "The Monster of Lake Tota." HIRARA: 'WHERE THE WORDS' October 21, 2013. Accessed May 01, 2016. https://josebaezg.wordpress.com/2013/10/21/el-monstruo-del-lago-de-tota/. Translated by Google Translate.
4. Eugenia Villa Posse. *Mitos Y Leyedas De Columbia*. Vol. II. Quito: Diego De Atienz a Y Av. Améric a, 1993.
5. Rodrigo Valenzuela San Martin. "Lake Tota Monster." Críptidos Y Fantasía. July 18, 2014. Accessed May 01, 2016. http://criptidosyfantasia.blogspot.com/2014/07/el-monstruo-del-lago-de-tota-un.html. Translated by Google Translate.
6. San Martin, "Lake Tota Monster."
7. Jose Baez, "The Monster of Lake Tota."
8. San Martin, "Lake Tota Monster."
9. Ibid.

Nguruvilú

1. Eberhart, *Mysterious Creatures: A Guide to Cryptozoology*, 220.
2. Austin Whittall. *Monsters of Patagonia: A Guide to Its Giants, Dwarves, Lake Creatures and Mythical Beasts*. (Las Vegas: Zagier & Urruty Publications, 2013), 159.
3. Whittall, *Monsters of Patagonia: A Guide to Its Giants, Dwarves, Lake Creatures and Mythical Beasts,* 159.
4. Ibid., 161.

Maripill

1. Whittall, *Monsters of Patagonia: A Guide to Its Giants, Dwarves, Lake Creatures and Mythical Beasts,* 161-162.

Water Tigers

1. Eberhart, *Mysterious Creatures: A Guide to Cryptozoology,* 581.
2. Michael Newton. "Stellar's Sea Cow." In *Hidden Animals: A Field Guide to Batsquatch, Chupacabra, and Other Elusive Creatures.* (Santa Barbara, CA: Greenwood Press, 2009), 50.
3. Eberhart, *Mysterious Creatures: A Guide to Cryptozoology,* 308.
4. Newton, *Hidden Animals: A Field Guide to Batsquatch, Chupacabra, and Other Elusive Creatures,* 50.
5. Vaudrey, Glen. "Blog 10: French Guiana." Still on the Track. March 10, 2011. Accessed June 22, 2016. http://forteanzoology.blogspot.com/2011_03_10_archive.html.
6. Eberhart, *Mysterious Creatures: A Guide to Cryptozoology,* 243.
7. Bernard Heuvelmans. "The Patagonian Giant Sloth." Translated by Richard Garnett. In *On the Track of Unknown Animals,* 3rd ed. (New York: Rutledge, 2014), 322-327.
8. Eberhart, *Mysterious Creatures: A Guide to Cryptozoology,* 603.

Camahueto

1. "Camahueto." Fundi2|Everything Chilean. 2012. Accessed February 22, 2016. https://fundi2.com/2012/03/09/camahueto/.
2. "Camahueto." Myths and Legends from Chiloé. Accessed February 22, 2016. http://mandradey.wix.com/myths#!en-blanco/c1sm5.
3. Everything Chilean, "Camahueto."

Mermaid Legends of South America

1. "Iara Mermaid in Mythology." Real Mermaids. Accessed February 23, 2016. http://www.realmermaids.net/mermaid-legends/iara-mermaid/
2. Real Mermaids, "Iara Mermaid in Mythology."
3. "Mermaids from South America." Tales of Faerie. June 17, 2015. Accessed February 23, 2016. http://talesoffaerie.blogspot.com/2015/06/mermaids-from-south-america.html
4. "Old and New Mermaids, Superstitions, Etc." *Asiatic Journal,* January 1823, 51-52. Accessed February 23, 2016. Google Books.

Man-eating Fish

1. Pablo Lehmann, Lucas J. Schvambach, and Roberto E. Reis, *A New Species of the Armored Catfish Parotocinclus (Loricariidae: Hypoptopmatinae), from the Amazon Basin in Columbia,* PDF, Neotropical Ichthyology, 2015.
2. "New 'Jaguar' Catfish Species Found in Amazon," LiveScience,, accessed July 24, 2016, http://www.livescience.com/30196-new-species-catfish-amazon-river.html.
3. Carol Kaesuk Yoon. "Amazon's Depths Yield Strange New World Of Unknown Fish." The New York Times. February 17, 1997. Accessed July 24, 2016. http://www.nytimes.com/1997/02/18/science/amazon-s-depths-yield-strange-new-world-of-unknown-fish.html.
4. Yoon, "Amazon's Depths Yield Strange New World of Unknown Fish."
5. Percy Harrison Fawcett. *Exploration Fawcett; Arranged from His Manuscripts, Letters, Log-books, and Records.* London: Hutchinson, 1953.

6. "Giant Catfish' Attacks Perkins Boy." NewsOK.com. August 16, 1985. Accessed July 24, 2016. http://newsok.com/article/2118087.

7. Josh Ward, "Bathers Beware: Giant Catfish Terrorizes Swimmers at Berlin Lake." SPIEGEL ONLINE, June 4, 2008, accessed July 24, 2016, http://www.spiegel.de/international/zeitgeist/bathers-beware-giant-catfish-terrorizes-swimmers-at-berlin-lake-a-557636.html.

8. *Tuscaloosa News* (Tuscaloosa), October 28, 1974.

9. "Hungarian Lake Catfish Attacks Fisherman." UPI. August 5, 2009.

10. George Keate. "Nessie Hunter Solves Monster Mystery." The Times. July 16, 2015. Accessed July 24, 2016. http://www.thetimes.co.uk/tto/environment/wildlife/article4499438.ece.

11. Mkassa2. "MonsterQuest Giant Killer Fish - National Geographic Documentary." YouTube. August 17, 2014. Accessed July 24, 2016. http://www.youtube.com/watch?v=D6vd4m3j-bg.

12. "Piraiba Fresh Water Monsters." Bass Fishing Gurus. 2015. Accessed July 24, 2016. http://www.bassfishing-gurus.com/piraiba-fresh-water-monsters/.

13. Tim Dinsdale, *The Leviathans* (London: Routledge & K. Paul, 1966), 113–115.

14. *The Aquarist and Pondkeeper*. Cornell University. Volumes 34–35, 1969, p182. https://books.google.com/books?id=AztMAAAAYAAJ.

15. Christine MacDonald. "Green Going Gone: The Tragic Deforestation of the Chaco." Rolling Stone. July 28, 2014. Accessed July 24, 2016. http://www.rollingstone.com/culture/news/green-going-gone-the-tragic-deforestation-of-the-chaco-20140728.

The Ahuizotl

1. Carol Rose. *Giants, Monsters, and Dragons: An Encyclopedia of Folklore, Legend, and Myth*. (New York: W.W. Norton & Company, 2000), 8.

2. "The Ahuizotl." The Aztecs at Mexicolore. Accessed May 15, 2016. http://www.mexicolore.co.uk/aztecs/aztefacts/ahuizotl.

Lake Atitlán

1. Aaron Roth. "The Monster of Lake Atitlan." Aaron Roth Stories and Monthly Newsletters from Latin America. January 17, 2011. Accessed March 13, 2016. http://www.aaronroth.net/2011/01/17/the-monster-of-lake-atitlan/.

2. "Divers Probe Mayan Ruins Submerged in Guatemala Lake." Reuters. October 30, 2009. Accessed March 13, 2016. http://www.reuters.com/article/us-guatemala-archaeology-idUSTRE59T4P120091030.

3. Reuters, "Divers Probe Mayan Ruins Submerged in Guatemala Lake."

4. Jeff Toorish. "Mayans, Myths, and Monsters." Advanced Diver Magazine. Accessed March 13, 2016. http://www.advanceddivermagazine.com/articles/atitlan/atitlan.html.

5. Roth, "The Monster of Lake Atitlan."

Lake Nicaragua

1. "The Bull Sharks of Lake Nicaragua." Nicaragua.com. Accessed March 13, 2016. http://www.nicaragua.com/blog/the-bull-sharks-of-lake-nicaragua.

2. Nicaragua.com, "The Bull Sharks of Lake Nicaragua."

3. Brent Swancer. "Way Out of Place Aquatic Beasts. Mysterious Universe. April 14, 2014. Accessed March 13, 2016. http://mysteriousuniverse.org/2014/04/way-out-of-place-aquatic-beasts/.

The Wihwin

1. Fletcher S. Bassett. "The Gods, Saints, and Demons of the Sea: Nick and Davey Jones, the Virgin." In *Legends and Superstitions of the Sea and of Sailors: In All Lands and at All Times.* (Chicago: Belford, Clarke, & Co., 1885), 93.
2. Alexander Porteous. "Forest Folklore, Mythology, and Romance." In *The Lore of the Forest.* (New York: Cosimo, 2005), 146.
3. Ben Johnson. "The Kelpie." Historic UK. Accessed March 30, 2016. http://www.historic-uk.com/CultureUK/The-Kelpie/.

Panama Monster

1. Virginia Wheeler. "Mystery Beast Terrified Kids." The Sun. September 17, 2009. Accessed May 12, 2016. http://www.thesun.co.uk/sol/homepage/news/2642152/Mystery-beast-terrified-kids.html.
2. "Kids Kill Panama 'Montauk Monster' by Lake." Perth Now. September 18, 2009. Accessed May 12, 2016. http://www.perthnow.com.au/news/world/kids-kill-panama-montauk-monster-by-lake/story-e6frg1p3-1225776476121.
3. Wheeler, "Mystery Beast Terrified Kids."
4. Sabrina Valle. "Panama 'Alien' Really a Dead, Bloated Sloth." National Geographic. November 9, 2009.
5. Valle, "Panama 'Alien' Really a Dead, Bloated Sloth."

Chan

1. John Kirk. *In the Domain of the Lake Monsters.* (Toronto: Key Porter Books, 1998),209.
2. Marcianitos Verdes, "EL MONSTRUO DEL LOCH NESS. LOS PRIMOS DE NESSIE," Marcianitos Verdes, July 20, 2008, accessed August 13, 2016, http://marcianitosverdes.haaan.com/2008/07/el-monstruo-del-loch-ness-los-primos-de-nessie-23/.
3. Kirk, *In the Domain of the Lake Monsters,* 210.
4. Ibid., 210-211.
5. "Category Archives: Mexican Cultural Stories." Surviving Mexico. Accessed March 06, 2016. http://survivingmexico.com/category/mexican-cultural-stories/.

Acámbaro Figurines

1. Charles Hapgood and David Hatcher Childress. *Mystery in Acambaro.* (Kempton, IL: Adventures Unlimited Press, 2000), 13-14.
2. Don Patton. "The Dinosaur Figurines of Acambaro, Mexico." http://www.bible.ca/tracks/tracks-acambaro.htm. Accessed June 13, 2016.
3. Patton, "The Dinosaur Figurines of Acambaro, Mexico."
4. Ibid.

The Yacumama in Mexico & Central America?

1. Eberhart, *Mysterious Creatures: A Guide to Cryptozoology,* 690.
2. Ibid., 359.

Lusca

1. "Blue Holes - Lairs of the Lusca." Search of Life. January 29, 2014. Accessed February 16, 2016. http://searchoflife.com/blue-holes-lairs-of-the-lusca-2014-01-29
2. Search of Life, "Blue Holes – Lairs of the Lusca.
3. Roy P. Mackal. "Biochemical Analyses of Preserved Octopus giganteus Tissue." *Cryptozoology*, 1986. 55–62.

The Creature from San Miguel Lagoon

1. "Mystery Monster." *The Dispatch* (Lexington), August 23, 1971.
2. "Mystery Monster." *The Dispatch*.
3. Mario Masvidal Saavedra. "The Creature from the San Miguel Lagoon." OnCuba. May 24, 2012. Accessed February 15, 2016. http://oncubamagazine.com/magazine-articles/creature-san-miguel-lagoon/.
4. "Mystery Monster." *The Dispatch*.

Huilla

1. Eberhart, *Mysterious Creatures: A Guide to Cryptozoology*, 239.
2. Dale A. Drinnon. "'Little Gold Sea Monster' No Longer Alone." Frontiers of Zoology. May 4, 2012. Accessed August 13, 2016. http://frontiersofzoology.blogspot.com/2012/05/little-gold-sea-monster-no-longer-alone.html.
3. Eberhart, *Mysterious Creatures: A Guide to Cryptozoology*, 239.

The Caribbean Monk Seal

1. M. P. Stanfield and I. L. Boyd. "Circumstantial Evidence for the Presence of Monk Seals in the West Indies." *Onyx* 32, 1998.

Some Monsters that weren't

1. Carol Rose. *Giants, Monsters, and Dragons: An Encyclopedia of Folklore, Legend, and Myth.* (New York: W.W. Norton & Company, 2000), 255.
2. Daniel Cohen. *Monsters, Giants, and Little Men from Mars: An Unnatural History of the Americas.* (Garden City, NY: Doubleday, 1975), 1-3.
3. Austin Whittall. "Chilean Harpy." Patagonian Monsters. April 27, 2010. Accessed May 05, 2016. http://patagoniamonsters.blogspot.com/2010/04/chilean-harpy.html.
4. Rose, *Giants, Monsters, and Dragons,* 255.
5. Whittall, *Monsters of Patagonia: A Guide to Its Giants, Dwarves, Lake Creatures and Mythical Beasts,* 203.
6. Darren Naish, "Whatever Happened to the Tecolutla Monster?," Tetrapod Zoology, July 10, 2008. Accessed August 01, 2016, http://scienceblogs.com/tetrapodzoology/2008/07/10/tecolutla-monster-carcass/.
7. John A. Keel, *The Complete Guide to Mysterious Beings* (New York: Doubleday, 1994), 293-294.
8. Naish, "Whatever Happened to the Tecolutla Monster?"

Some Final Observations

1. Jess Swanson. "Discovery Channel Documentary Confirms 70-Year-Old Legend of Cuban 'Monster Shark.'" Miami New Times. July 06, 2015. Accessed August 13, 2016. http://www.miaminewtimes.com/news/discovery-channel-documentary-confirms-70-year-old-legend-of-cuban-monster-shark-7731095.

Index

About the Author

Denver Michaels is an author with a passion for cryptozoology, the paranormal, lost civilizations, and all things unexplained. At age 42, the Virginia native released his first book *People are Seeing Something*—a culmination of many years of research on the lake monster phenomenon.

Michaels is employed as an engineering technologist and works full-time. He is married with three children. In his spare time, he continues to perform research and writing for future works.

Figure 26: The author in Peru.

Favorite me at Smashwords:
https://www.smashwords.com/profile/view/denvermichaels

Follow me on Twitter: http://twitter.com/_denvermichaels

Like my Facebook page: http://facebook.com/ denvermichaels1213

Visit my website: http://www.denvermichaels.net

www.ingramcontent.com/pod-product-compliance
Lightning Source LLC
Chambersburg PA
CBHW060626290526
45793CB00001B/154